Money Magic

Lynne Palmer

ISBN 0-9652296-0-2

First Printing 1987

Published by:

Lynne Palmer
Toll Free: 1-800-615-3352
Web Site: www.lynnepalmer.com
Email: lynnepalmer@lynnepalmer.com

Printed and bound in the United States of America

INTRODUCTION

Do you think you are lucky? If you don't, you had better start reprogramming your thoughts. You've heard about King Midas and that all he touched turned to gold. Wouldn't it be wonderful if you had the same capabilities? It's not impossible. Anything that the mind can conceive, can happen. Those who have made fortunes have been lucky because they **know the secret** of going after their dreams. They have that "magic" or "Midas" touch. There is "Magic" when it comes to making lots of money. In my opinion it is within *your power* to be as affluent as you want, if you apply the procedures outlined in this book.

Ari Onassis, Henry Kaiser, Billy Rose, Madonna and others started at the bottom and worked their way up to being either multimillionaires or billionaires—a "rags to riches" saga. What kind of power did they possess? Wouldn't you love to be able to harness that power and be rich too?

The science of astrology has been around for centuries. The shepherds tending their flocks discovered it, royalty used it by having their own court astrologer, and in modern times over 50 million people in the United States are followers of astrology. The ancient astrologers were alchemists. They knew how to transmute metals into gold and silver. They kept these secrets hidden in symbol form and have passed them down through esoteric manuscripts from the dark ages to this century where they have come to light. They used candles and incantations such as I have mentioned in this book. Magical devices such as: gimmicks, affirmations, positive thoughts, good relationships and a little luck—all help bring you material rewards.

Through the years, I have helped thousands of people increase their income, or make a fortune. There were those negative people who didn't listen and, to this day, do not yet understand what they did wrong. Some have the knack to change and be positive all the time—they are the winners. The losers, are doubters and get negative. I will guide you in this *Money Magic* book so you'll take the steps that will lead to your catching the brass ring. It is all within *YOU* to be rich. So why not give it a try? Confidence and belief can make you a winner just like champion athletes have proven when they won a Gold Medal or any other award. So Good Luck! And let me hear from you, when you see the riches rolling in.

CHAPTER ONE
Money Devices and Affirmations

Sandalwood incense is burning in a darkened garage room. A middle-aged man makes an imaginary circle with his right hand, which engulfs an altar with a red, white and yellow candle and the spot where he stands during the ritual. He lights a yellow candle, touches the silver pendant hanging from his neck and hovers over the candle, repeating an incantation, "I deliver this candle to Methuselah. Bring me money because I need it to pay the doctor's bills and the rent, to buy food for my wife, children and myself. Oh, Methuselah you are ever so wise and kind, please answer my prayers for money." And now his voice becomes loud and filled with deep conviction while he lights the red candle. "I deliver this candle to San Juan de Conquistador. I am delivering this candle so you can bring me money I just asked for (a deep breath is taken as he raises his hand upward toward the roof) so that I can conquer all of the opposition to my success." The Lord's Prayer is then repeated three times. The unlit white candle on the altar is now lit and with half-closed eyes he states, "I dedicate this candle to my spirit guides and guardian angels. I evoke and deliver this candle so I will have the strength to overcome my crisis by giving me an uplifting spirit. And I ask you to bring a miracle into my life in the direction desired. So shall it be!"

A buddy had told Bill J. (an Aquarian), that by lighting a yellow candle (yellow is for Venus, the planet ruling ready cash) he could attract the money he needed to remedy his financial difficulties. His friend said that if he burned green candles Bill could attract money as well. But because Bill needed cash immediately he did his magic incantations with a yellow candle. His pal told him that a red candle would give him the strength to fight and conquer his opposition (red is for Mars), and the white candle would bring him extra help from his spirit guides and guardian angles (white is for purity, and the planet Uranus).

Does it work? In my opinion magic is in the believing. Whatever thoughts a person holds strongly, vividly imagines to be true, ardently desires, sincerely believes in, and enthusiastically acts upon *can* work. But it is all up to the individual. I have seen hundreds of cases where it did work, but again, I could say that perhaps the results were because the individual was under fortunate planetary influences. Who knows? I have only the evidence as it's presented to me by my clients and acquaintances, and the conclusions I've drawn from my own experiments. In many cases the person was *not* under lucky astrological influences, and *still succeeded* through these "*magical devices*".

The dictionary defines magic as "Seeming control over or foresight of natural events, forces, etc., by the ritual invocation of supernatural agencies; also, the practice of this control. Magic involves the belief that man can coerce nature by the use of certain rites, formulas, actions, etc. It can be found as an element in all primitive religions."

Also positive thinking attracts success in money ventures but that is dealt with in another chapter. Meanwhile, think of money magic as a new game that could pay off in handsome rewards. Or think of it as an additional way to become prosperous, okay?

There are many types of "magical devices" but the principles are identical. All thoughts are released into space; once released (don't hang on to them, let them go—that's what release means) they will return to the sender. Don't hold negative thoughts at the time for that's what will bounce back at you. Always think positive.

Every time you handle any kind of currency—cash, check, money order or credit cards—be sure to repeat, "God (the Creator) multiplies this money now and continues to do so forever." This statement helps to multiply your money.

The *Check* "magical device" is one of my favorites and works wonderfully well. It's very simple, but you need a checking account at a bank for the best results. However, many people have written it on a piece of paper instead of a regular check—and it worked successfully for them. Yellow paper is the best because yellow vibrates to Venus, the planet that has rulership over ***ready cash***. Take your business or personal check and fill it out as follows, or on a piece of yellow paper in the form of a check. You can also write this for someone else. In so doing you replace your name with the person's name.

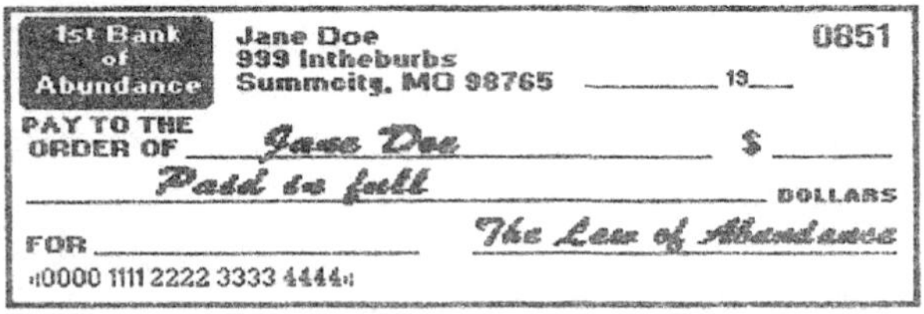
1st Bank of Abundance
Jane Doe
939 Intheburbs
Summcity, MO 98765
0851
_______ 19___
PAY TO THE ORDER OF Jane Doe $ ______
Paid in full DOLLARS
FOR ______________ The Law of Abundance
⑆0000 1111 2222 3333 4444⑆

Figure 1

On the check or paper leave the date and dollars lines blank. If you write in the amount of money desired, you'll limit yourself to said amount. If you write in the date, the check will only be good for that date. *The Law of Abundance* is written where your signature normally is signed. It is *The Law of Abundance* that is going to pay you (Jane Doe) in full (that is why Paid In Full is written on one of the lines).

Do **not** void the check stub or you'll void the check. Instead just write in "for the Law of Abundance". After completing the instructions, fold the check in half, place in your wallet or checkbook, and forget it. Once you've written this Law of Abundance check, you do not have to repeat it unless you change bank accounts or just want to do it every month.. You can do the *Check* "magical device" as many times as you like. However, there is a time to write the check...twenty-four hours **after the New Moon** (although the week that follows is still a good time to write it). The idea is that as the Moon **increases in light** (from new moon to full moon). so **does your money**. The closer to the New Moon date, the better. However, do *NOT DO THIS ON THE NEW MOON* nor three days before the Full Moon nor after the Full Moon...it will not work in you favor, if you do.

If you do not want to hide this in your wallet or checkbook, then paste or tape the folded check under your telephone (if your business is dependent on the phone), or hide it in important certificates (bonds, C.D.'s from the bank, stocks, contracts), your safety deposit box, or anywhere in your house or office.

If you repeat the *Check* "magical device" (some people do it once a month), do NOT tear up or throw out the old check, or paper — unless you change your bank account. Do not dwell on the Law of Abundance check. You must forget about it so the energy can be released to bring you in the money; perhaps the money will be the result of a refund, rebate, lottery or gambling win, insurance money or extra bonus you had not expected. Do not try to figure where the money is coming from (this defeats your purpose). Just think that The Law of Abundance is always going to pay you in full. Do not write this check at the wrong phase of the Moon or you will be like the people who wrote me saying that they didn't reap any benefits because they really believed they could do it any time.

Through the years I have told people about this *Check* "magical device" over the radio, in books, classes, workshops, and to clients, friends and acquaintances; the results have been phenomenal when instructions were carefully followed. In June 1984 I appeared on the Baltimore, Maryland *People Are Talking* TV show hosted by Oprah Winfrey and Richard Schere. I gave the public instructions about how to write the Law of Abundance check. One of the viewers told her next door neighbor about it. The couple wrote the Law of Abundance check and within a week won the Million Dollar Lottery! In July 1984 they appeared on the *People Are Talking* TV show and attributed their luck to my *Check* "magical device".

There was another million dollar winner, Russell W—, of Arizona. There have been may people, prior to and after these fortunate big winners, who (after they wrote the "*Check* magical device") have won small amounts of money on the lottery, Bingo and other games of chance. On numerous occasions I appeared on the Cleveland, Ohio TV show *Morning Exchange*. After my first appearance there, the station had so many calls that the WEWS-TV station had an extremely large version of a check drawn so they could show it to viewers so they would do it properly (this check was shown repeatedly long after my initial appearance and again after other appearances). The *Morning Exchange* show has a "call-in" line while the show is being aired. On my other appearances there many of the callers told how after shortly writing the Law of Abundance check they won at Bingo or received refunds, a raise in pay, rebates and money from various areas.

Joyce Vincent, a client of mine who lived in New York City. held the Law of Abundance check in her hand and forcefully stated, "Come on Law of Abundance check! Make me a winner of the Wingo newspaper contest!" Soon thereafter, she won $50,000 which she had to share.

One of my ex-students, Gary Z., had been on unemployment for quite some time. Gary heard about the *Check* "magical device" from me when he attended one of my classes. A few weeks later he called and excitedly exclaimed, "My whole life has changed since I did the Law of Abundance check. I'm never without money where previously days would go by and I wouldn't have a cent on me. Now, just as I got low on money, a refund check arrived; prior to that I received a rebate from Internal Revenue, and a friend of mine paid me back a loan I made ten years ago! It has all been unbelievable! And to top it all off, I start a job that pays a great salary!"

A Virgo client, Beverly R., told me that after she wrote the Law of Abundance check an Insurance company called her and said that they had been in the process of switching to a computer program and in do doing discovered her misplaced policy. Beverly had forgotten all about the policy, and was in complete shock when the man informed her that her paid-up policy had matured fifteen years ago, and the company owed her four thousand dollars!

Many years ago I appeared on a radio show in San Francisco and mentioned the Law of Abundance check. About a year later I received a long-distance phone call from a Pisces, Mrs. Roberta J., who complimented me for my help by mentioning the Law of Abundance check on the radio. It had worked very well for her, but her Capricorn friend Gertrude S. was confused by an incident that had occurred as a result of writing the *Check* "magical device". Roberta was calling me for an explanation.

It seems that after Roberta heard me on the radio, she excitedly called Gertrude, who was having financial difficulties. Mrs. J. forgot to tell Gertrude that she was not to write in the date or the amount. Gertrude was so elated that she immediately dated the check and wrote in a small amount (around two hundred dollars).

That afternoon Gertrude went to the supermarket, did her shopping, and on the way out stopped at a vending machine; she put the proper amount of money in the slot, and, to her amazement, out came all the money that was stored in the machine. It was like being in Las Vegas and hitting the jackpot on a slot machine! Gertrude hastily looked around to see if anyone had seen what had happened. No one had, so she quickly shoved all the money into her grocery bags and got out of there as fast as she could. When Gertrude got home, she counted the money and lo and behold, it added up to the exact sum she had written on the Law of Abundance check!

As the result of this Gertrude wholeheartedly believed in the *Check* "magic device". She kept waiting for something more to happen, but her finances didn't improve, they got worse! And that's why Roberta was calling me to ask what had gone wrong. I explained that Gertrude should not have limited herself by writing the date or amount on the check because that was the only date it could be used for. I told Roberta to tell Gertrude to tear up the old check, wait for another week (when there would be a new Moon) and start all over again, but *without* the date or amount on the check!

The *Play-Money* "magical device" isn't as good as the Law of Abundance check because it limits your money. You've all heard that if you pray for a certain amount, you always get half? However, if you wish to demonstrate your luck with this *Play-Money* "magical device" buy packets of play money at the dime store and hide it all over your home or office. Hide it in books, important papers, behind objects, or under them (including the paper lining used in drawers or tape the play money underneath your telephone).

By surrounding yourself with money you feel happy, optimistic, and wealthy. It is this feeling of confidence and well-being that attracts money to you. Have you ever noticed that when money is coming in you are happy, carefree, and want to enjoy life? And the moment you worry, tighten up your purse strings, or stop living it up, the flow of money stops?

The sign Sagittarius and its ruler, the planet Jupiter, represent wealth, abundance, fun and pleasure; increases come through their influence. At the opposite extreme is the sign Capricorn and its ruler, the planet Saturn, which represents poverty, want, discontent, and sorrow; decreases come through their influence.

From the preceding you can see why it's important to try to act and think in accordance with the Sagittarius and Jupiter traits, rather than the Capricorn and Saturn ones. That is why people who express Capricorn and/or Saturn traits need to surround themselves with riches, even though it may only be "play money" they temporarily change their attitude and thus attract money. But if you, for one moment, disbelieve (remember, magic is in the believing) and become negative—this, or any other "magical device" will not work fully in your behalf! The more positive the mood, the more positive the results! Positive attitudes attract positive things; negative attitudes attract negative results!

I told Anne G. about the **Check** and **Play-Money** magical devices. The next day she went to work, wrote the Law of Abundance check on a business account, and called me frantically wondering what she should do with the stub. I told Anne, "Don't void the stub because that action will void the money; instead write on the stub that it's for the Law of Abundance—but leave the date off."

Anne said, "But what shall I tell the accountant when he asks what this is for?"

"Oh," I remarked, "just tell him the truth. Maybe he'll want to do it for himself!"

Later in the day Anne bought five million dollars in play money, took it to the office, and hid it everywhere. Her coworkers thought she had flipped! Luckily Anne's boss was out of town for a few weeks or she might have lost her job!

Within a few weeks the owner of the business returned to a scene that left him flabbergasted! The business was jumping—orders were coming in so fast the employees couldn't fill them right away; temporary help had to be hired. They ran out of goods and had to reorder over and over again. The hectic pace continued and the money is still rolling in, after a decade! I ask you was it the "Law of

Abundance check" the *Play-Money* "magical device," fate, or was it all in the stars?

The *Play-Money* "magical device" and the *Seed-Money* "magical device" use the same principle, except that "seed money" is real money. There are many people, including a few friends of mine, who save "seed money." The idea is that the more you have saved, the more you will attract. The same principle applies; to a savings account, but those who save *Seed-Money,* swear that it's superior to a savings account because it is on or around you all of the time, thus attracting it directly to you that much faster! However, the drawback is that you lose interest in money that the bank would be paying you, if you had this money in a savings account. Plus, it can be dangerous in case of theft in your abode.

A Leo friend of mine saves *Seed-Money* and she also has a savings account in the bank. I wonder which one was really doing the work to attract the money—perhaps, both! I know a Scorpio woman who saved thirty thousand dollars in *Seed-Money* and did not have any bank amount, until recently. I talked her into opening a savings account because of the danger of bring robbed with all that cash hidden all over her townhouse. Not even her husband knew about it! The money she saved was from the allowance her husband gave her for household expenses. It took years of wise shopping to accumulate the thirty thousand dollars she hid.

I know two women who carry their *Seed-Money* in a hanky folded up in their bras. As their money increases, they change it to larger denominations. Once they have a certain amount saved, they put it in the bank, leaving just enough in the brassiere to start(plant) a new "seed". If the didn't, they'd have bulging cleavage!

Both of these ladies (one is in her eighties) feel safe hiding the money in their bras. They both believe that no one would ever suspect they had money hidden there. They dare anyone, especially a strange man or robber, to get fresh with them! "I don't trust the money anyplace, except on me." said one lady. "I'll smack a man on the head if he tries to come near my breast area!" she defiantly exclaims. If you venture to guess that both are Capricorns, you are right!

Another popular *Money* "magical device" involves using a *Bible* to attract whatever you want: Fold a white piece of lined paper into the shape of a triangle; make sure the bottom half (the part opposite the point) is folded so it meets the bottom ends of the point part. If your bottom part sticks out (about an inch) on the left and right sides, it is to be expected.

On the inside part of the triangle (pyramid shape) list whatever you want (money marriage, job, etc.) and refold; place the folded triangle in the Bible on the same page as the twenty-third Psalm. The folded written part should be face

15

down on the Bible's printed words, with the point part on the triangle pointed outward.

Every day READ the twenty-third, twenty-fourth and thirty-seventh Psalms. Don't open the triangular piece of paper unless you are adding to the list or deleting something from it. You can add things from time to time (but make sure it's after the new Moon or within the week that follows—look in the newspaper for the New Moon date). You can delete things if you no longer care to attract them, or if some of your wishes have already been fulfilled.

This method is very effective; however, patience and persistence are required because it takes a while for it to work. One client of mine, Robert T. (a Taurus), longed to appear on a certain television show, so he wrote the name of the show on the list and placed it in the Bible. Robert wrote a book which was published and, two years after his request was written in the Bible, he appeared on the TV show he wanted. Leave it to a Taurus to be patient and wait for it to happen!

Next there's the *Pyramid* "magical device". This trick involves seed money or play money or the Law of Abundance check. It utilizes a small (one foot or higher) pyramid. Place the open part of the pyramid facing east in a part of the house that isn't frequented much. **Never** allow anyone to touch your *Pyramid*, *Play* or *Seed Money*.

There are all sizes of pyramids from the gigantic ones in Egypt to small ones used in a home or office. It has been written that pyramids are a source of energy which radiate light, electricity, magnetism and heat, although often a pyramid does not seem to radiate any energy. There are many theories of how a pyramid operates as well as many case histories relating to the astounding results people have had with them. The researchers have consistently reported these "happenings" in books and magazine articles. Those who use them swear plants grow better when placed inside a pyramid; others say that seeds improve their germination when put in the interior of a pyramid. And then there are those who believe that when actual cash is placed within a pyramid the money they have in their wallet or bank account multiplies.

Pyramids are not easy to find. Try your luck at a magic shop, health food store or places which sell books and objects related to the occult. Make one of your own out of cardboard, poster board, glass or mirror. Cut the material you use into three triangular sides. Place these sides in a slanted position so they all reach a point at the top center. Glue them to each other and glue all three to a base (the floor of your pyramid). Leave an opening in the front (The back side is slanted like the two sides and is placed opposite the open side.) Those pyramids made of glass or mirror are supposedly superior to those made of other materials because they reflect the contents thus emanating more power to attract the desired object. If the cutting of glass or mirror is not your "cup of tea," perhaps you can pay a glass maker to make one for you.

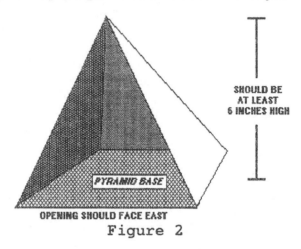

SHOULD BE
AT LEAST
6 INCHES HIGH

PYRAMID BASE

OPENING SHOULD FACE EAST

Figure 2

Place the pyramid in a room or window sill. Make sure that the open part faces *east* because the Sun rises in the east and that's when the rays are the most powerful for "magic." In fact you should always face east when performing a magic ceremony. Twenty-four hours after the New Moon place your *Seed Money*, *Play Money* or the *Law of Abundance Check* inside the pyramid. If at another time you want to energize more money, or anything else, do it in cycles of three (three sides to the pyramid)—three days, three weeks or three months. You can leave the contents inside the pyramid in cycles of three—three days, weeks, months or years.

For about three years I experimented with the play money hidden all over the apartment and in the pyramid. For the first year this was effective. Two years later I switched from the play money to the seed money in the pyramid. This worked a little better than the play money but it made me nervous having cash in my apartment. Then I realized that I was limiting what I could attract because in both cases I had set sums of money in the pyramid. The seed money was put into the bank and the play money was gathered from drawers, books, contracts and placed in a big bundle (millions of dollars in play money) hidden away. I wrote another Law of Abundance check and placed it in the pyramid. From that time on there has been a noticeable, almost startling difference. The Law of Abundance check in the pyramid is more effective than anything else that I've experimented with.

Another *Money* "magical device" is the *Wish List*. Many of my clients and ex-students find that within twenty-four hours their wishes came true. I've found this very rewarding through the last several decades. When you are alone, write on a piece of paper the things you want. For example: I want to increase my finances. I want two hundred dollars a month raise. I wish to own a home on ___ street. I want a Cadillac car. I want a speed boat. I want a C.D. player. I want a new TV set. I want a diamond ring—carats. I want a mink coat. I want a promotion. I want to be famous. I want to marry ___ (person). I want to travel all over the world.

List as many things as you desire. Usually the first time you make a list, it is quite lengthy, which is perfectly acceptable. In time, your needs, wants and desires change thus alter your *Wish List* when this occurs. Add to the list when you want something new and delete those wishes that were granted. *At the bottom of the list, write*; *"THANK YOU FOR MANIFESTING THESE THINGS IF THEY ARE FOR MY HIGHEST GOOD."* (You are thanking God, the Creator or whoever brings you your wishes.)

When you list each item on your *Wish List*, visualize that you already have it. Devote at least five minutes meditating on *each* wish. Pour love and warmth into your desires. Put strong—emotional feelings into your desire. Glow all over with warmth and radiate happiness as if your wish had come true. Let your imagination run wild. Realize that it is there for you and *IS YOURS*. Picture the car you want. Imagine you are driving it. Praise it for being beautiful and running smoothly. Visualize your boss giving you a raise. Dream about that diamond ring you want. Imagine that you're wearing your new mink coat to the swankiest affairs. Picture yourself traveling to the world's top resorts.

Once you've visualized a wish, do not repeat it. Have faith that God, the Creator or a higher-than-human power is going to provide you with your needs, wants and desires. However, the next day after you first wrote out your *Wish List*, read it when you wake up and just before you go to sleep. Do not think about it anymore. Release it to the cosmic forces (the ethers) and go about your life in the usual way. Do not tell anyone about it because that will make it difficult to attain your desires. You never know about the negative thoughts others may send your way.

The *Four-step-plan* is mental magic. Visualize both what you want *and* the results as you want them to take place. Do this in four stages: early evening before the day of the meeting, just before going to sleep the night before the meeting, and thirty minutes before the meeting. At the meeting glance into the person's eyes and mentally say those words you've said previously in the mental demonstration.

The *Four-step-plan* can be used with anyone or anything and under any conditions. Perhaps you want to get hired—use it for an interview. Or you want the banker to give you a loan, and so on. But after each step is completed *RELEASE THE ENERGY* so it can work. Think about something else. My friend Marylyn did this to get into a Broadway show. When she walked on-stage to audition she used the fourth step and mentally (as she quickly glanced into their eyes) said to the row of people sitting there—the producer, director and others—"Hire me!"

Another "magical device" is *Mirror Magic*. Stand in front of a mirror and make your requests. Be careful what you say when you look in a mirror because those words will bounce right back at you! Never say "I," instead say "You" when you look into a mirror. Praise yourself, such as, "*You* are beautiful (handsome)." "*You* are magnetic." "*You* are a great actor." "*You* are dynamic." "*You* are successful." Put a strong and positive emotion into your voice (like a command) when you make an affirmation. Speak as if a strong and forceful energy is surging through your entire body. Any type of 'magic' has more power to manifest when you follow this procedure.

Perhaps you will want to look in the mirror and say, "*You* are like a magnet drawing money to you!" Or "*You* are going to win the lottery!" Or "*You* are going to win the sweepstakes contest you entered." Or "*You* are going to get a salary increase!" Or '*Your* stocks are going up, up, up!" Or "The property *you* own is increasing in value!" Or "*You* are going to sell your home for a lot of money." Or, "_____ (name of person) loves *you*."

NOTE: Start all *Mirror Magic* affirmations after the New Moon or up to three days before the Full Moon. Affirmations may be repeated whenever desired, however, it is best to release the energy into the ethers and go about your daily duties. If you make an affirmation *WITHOUT LOOKING IN THE MIRROR*, always say "I," i.e., "*I* am like a magnet drawing money to me."

The *Floating-cash* "magical device" is easy to do...visualize real greenbacks floating down from your ceiling and covering you, your household goods, office machinery or equipment. This is a "magical device" that can increase your money. The idea is for you to feel so rich that you are inundated with all this money, thus, making it easier to attract like amount.

Gambling: Those lucky people who win are usually confident and feel they are going to win the million dollar lottery or the five million dollar sweepstakes. When they go to a gambling casino they are usually in a happy frame of mind—it is that surety that makes them a winner, plus Lady Luck is smiling at them. Often a person will feel "the dice are getting cold" and, luckily, quit the crap game while they are still ahead. Of course this is one's instinct (ESP, hunch, psychic feeling) giving the individual the clue to leave the dice alone or be ready to lose a bundle. Those who don't listen to their inner voice guiding them are usually sorry later. Therefore, always try to follow your "gut feeling."

When you receive a sweepstakes ticket in the mail it may read "____ (your name) could

23

be a $-------------- winner," scratch out the words "could be" so it will be as if you are the winner (this is the copy you are to keep). When you are filling out the sweepstakes entry form or lotto ticket) feel confident, happy and be enthusiastic—pretend as if you had just won the ten million dollar sweepstakes (or lottery). When you place the sweepstakes entry form in a mail box, say, "Thank you God for making me a winner!" (Always give thanks in advance and make believe it has already happened.) Put the sweepstakes stub (or the lottery ticket) away and forget about it, Thus, releasing the energy into the ethers to help bring it about.

Magic Ceremonies: You may want to do a special ritual to invoke more power to the object of your desire, i.e., money. Sandalwood incense is, supposedly, the best for this type of ceremony. You need a white candle, and "Success Oil" which can be bought at a Botanica in a Hispanic neighborhood. Or you can make your own Success Oil by mixing Mineral Oil and your favorite perfume together in a small bottle. Hide it and don't let anyone touch it. Once you've mixed these ingredients (the oil and perfume,) hold it in your two hands and empower it with thought of success. Don't forget to speak in a strong, positive, forceful and emotional voice. Visualize yourself as successful in all your undertakings. Once you do this, you do not have to repeat it when you use the Success Oil in the future ceremonies. Also always place a drop behind your ears and on any object you are magnetizing, i.e., "play money."

To Get What You Want; Twenty-four hours after the New Moon is the best time to initiate the following ceremony. Set a certain time every day, for a few days only, to perform your ritual. Be alone. Make an imaginary circle (with your right hand) around your enclosed area. In this space is incense, a white candle and Success Oil. Light the incense in its burner. Then ignite the white candle. Place Success Oil behind your ears and on the object you are magnetizing. If there isn't any object—it's a thing you want—then visualize yourself putting Success Oil on the project. If it is money that is desired—visualize it; see yourself with the cash in your hands, spending it, buying and decorating a home lavishly, purchasing furs, jewels, clothes or a car, yacht or business. Picture yourself happy and laughing as if you didn't have a care in the world. Pretend you are going to parties where famous people are in attendance. Imagine that you are traveling around the world. See yourself giving your loved one's money, setting your children up in business or with an education. Visualize that you are treating your pals to a wonderful night out—a trip—an expensive gift or something they've always dreamed of owning. Continue on with your day dreaming—pretend it *is* happening.

Thoughts Produce Things—so the stronger the thought, the easier it is to produce the desired object. And conclude your ceremony with the positive statement of "So shall it be!" Do **not** blow the candle out, let it burn out by itself—down to the wicker. Place the candle in a safe place, i.e., the kitchen sink. Use candles that burn quickly. Don't let other members of the family touch the candle or blow it out. Be secretive. You don't want negative thoughts from anyone to work against you. Be positive and remember that "Magic is in the believing!"

Here is an *Old Wives Tale*: "Never put your purse on the floor, or it'll be empty." I have noticed that when I abide by this adage, I don't spend as much and that my pocketbook is full of cash.

Another *Money Magic* tip is: when you pay someone with currency, fold the bill in half and hand it to the person with the unfolded ends on top. The other individual will take hold of the ends and as the money is being drawn from your hands—imagine that the other half that is folded and facing you IS coming back to you. (So money is going out but is returning to you too.) I've noticed that cash is recieved quicker whenever I do this. The best way is to experiment yourself. What do you have to lose? Nothing! But just think about what you could gain — your money back and maybe double!

Affirmations: Start all affirmations twenty-four hours after the New Moon and up to three days before the Full Moon. Say your affirmations daily at the same time—preferably, when you awaken in the morning, at twelve noon and at night before you go to sleep. Repeat affirmations daily for a few weeks to a month then release the energy so it can manifest. The moment you feel negative, start saying the affirmation again. Your affirmation may consist of short sentences or long paragraphs; however, using the same phrases repetitiously is best. Once they are said, spend the remainder of the day in your usual routine; thus, you'll have time to release the energy so the affirmation can occur, as well as have the time to take action and make things happen in your favor.

Through the years I have given the following *Affirmations* (which work the best because of the results which were reported to me) to my friends, clients, radio and television audiences and to strangers who had problems and showed their negativity when we met by chance at social functions.

"I am rich and getting richer. I am lucky and getting luckier. I am successful and getting more successful. I am a winner. I am happy and getting happier. There's money out there for me to make and there's no reason in the world why I can't get it.!"

"I *Golden Key* away all negative thoughts, conditions and situations. I free myself of restrictions and limitations." Or you may say, "My good is everywhere! (This statement is without limitation—it implies your good is with money, people, love, etc.). I move to my greater good. I am safe and secure."

It has been wonderful seeing the lives of people change from bad to good just by saying these affirmations—to me they are the best ones to express. However, here's a few that, also, have helped others: "Thanks for bringing me abundance and prosperity." "I am a good person and attract good unto myself and bring it to others." "I send out love to everyone." "I have confidence and am productive." "I am filled with kindness and use my knowledge to help others." "I have no fears and approach life with a positive attitude that all will turn out for the best." "I increase my power daily." "I find that I am at peace with those around me and understand the shortcomings of others." "I know that the peace I find with myself flows through my body giving me an abundance of vital energy." "I give thanks to the Creator that all my dreams can come true, especially, when I am patient, loving, and positive in my thoughts and actions to myself and my fellow man."

The Color Yellow: The ancients assigned certain colors to the zodiac signs and planets. Yellow, which I mentioned at the beginning of this chapter, is ruled by Venus and represents ready cash. Therefore surround yourself in yellow—wear it or display it in your living quarters (Toilet Paper, Kleenex, paper towels, sheets, bedspreads, dishes, etc.) Wear it or use it in the office (tape dispensers, paper, pencils, pens, etc.) Again, the magic is in the believing. So why not give it a try?

28

In my opinion all of these "Money-Magical devices" are effective ways to gain money. Mental Magic, likewise, can help you with a career or in business. With inflation on the rise, and with all the current economical problems, currency fluctuations, and the like—I think it's important to know and try these "magical devices". This is one way to get and stay ahead; and the other methods are to use positive thinking, wear your lucky color and apply astrology and numerology techniques to your daily life. And with the combination of everything, you're ahead of the game and could become rich quickly. And that's what it's all about, isn't it?

CHAPTER TWO
Colors

Are you aware that when you wear a color that is lucky for you, that you are tapping into your subconscious and stimulating powerful forces to attract wealth, success and happiness?

Colors, when worn (and in your surroundings), add energy to your subconscious thoughts. Thus, fortunate or unfortunate events occur depending upon whether they are lucky, or unlucky, for you. Negative thoughts (energies) attract discord and repel wealth. Positive thoughts (energies) attract harmony and wealth. If you have always been negative, it is difficult, although not impossible, to think positive thoughts. However, it is easier to be positive if your lucky color is used on your body or in your home or office environment. When all of these factors are harmonious, you feel more energetic and thus it is easier to counteract any discordant force you may encounter.

Do you know a lucky person? You've probably read or heard about people who seem to have Lady Luck smiling at them continually. Have you ever wondered, "Why can't I be lucky like — ? I am talented, intelligent and work hard. I just can't understand why I don't get the breaks." Perhaps, it's negative thinking that holds you back. Or perhaps it is the color of the clothes you wear that are contributing to your being left out of the life you've always dreamed about. A life of wealth, a beautiful home, car, boat, parties, clothes, furs, jewels and first-class travel to any destination— easy living. Therefore, if you try to improve your thinking and surround yourself with harmonious vibrations, you may be on the road to riches. It is all up to you. No one can do your thinking for you nor take the type of action which is necessary to attain these luxuries.

The following color guidelines should give you a clue as to what color clothes or accessories you should wear or have in your home or office environment; thus you can be lucky and enhance your chances of attracting money, success, love and happiness. Also given is the type of thinking and action which will help you attract the things you want.

Yellow or *Gold* clothes or accessories should be worn if you are depressed, insecure, fearful, worried, apprehensive, suspicious, negative or feel sorry for yourself. The *Yellow* clothes or accessories should make you feel light, happy, cheerful, energetic and kindly toward others. You may be more easy going and your social life may be on the increase, or you may take an interest in the arts. The *Gold* clothes or accessories should make you feel proud of yourself. You may glow, want to be on center stage, and your vitality increases. *Yellow* attracts **ready cash** and *Gold* attracts *Gold*.

> *Note*: Do **not** wear black, grey, blue or brown because these colors darken the spirits and increase negativity.

Black, Grey, Blue or **Dark Brown** clothes or accessories should be worn if you suffer with love because you're too kind, sweet and loving to the object of your affections. Also if you are lazy, take the easy way out, live only for fun and pleasure, and say "yes" to people when you really want to say "no." Also wear these colors if you daydream, give imaginary attributes to loved ones, procrastinate, or if deals and projects fall through or you get involved in get-rich-quick schemes, or others are deceptive and tell fibs.

The **Black, Grey, Blue** or **Dark Brown** clothes or accessories should make you calm, cool, collected, serious, ambitious, industrious, able to live on a schedule, stable, work hard, be aware of scams, face reality and say "no" to others. It will be easier to save money, invest wisely and plan for the future.

> *Note*: Do **not** wear yellow because you'll be counter-productive.

Purple clothes and accessories should be worn if you are nervous, confused, forgetful, or have difficulty concentrating, making decisions and expressing yourself through the written or spoken word. Also wear purple if you are high-strung, erratic, or experience difficulty handling the sudden shocks and upheavals which occur.

The *Purple* clothes or accessories should make you feel confident, optimistic, and give you faith that all your problems will be solved because everything is in divine order. You just may laugh your way through all of the surprises and radical changes, because you believe that everything happens for the best. It's this happy-go-lucky attitude, and prayer, that attracts wealth.

> *Note*: Do **not** wear white because it enhances the upsets and difficulties.

Violet clothes or accessories should be worn if you are heavy set, gaining weight, careless, overly optimistic, too confident or expect too much of others, make snap judgments or do things to excess.

The *Violet* clothes or accessories should make you feel less impulsive and enthusiastic. You may be able to weigh factors better because your reasoning powers have improved—you stop, think and analyze everything, thus it is easier to prevent actions based on faulty judgment. These attributes are an aid to becoming rich.

> *Note*: Do **not** wear purple or you'll be counter-productive.

Green clothes or accessories should be worn if you are accident prone, temperamental, impulsive and hasty in your actions, too pushy or get angry and irritable quickly.

The *Green* clothes or accessories should make you feel like helping others, making the home more enjoyable. You may be interested in comforting and nurturing others. Good deeds may be performed thus converting destructive energy into constructive action. Thus it's easier to build a large bank account. Drive a green automobile to counteract accidents. You may discover that you are moving slower and taking less chances with everything. Your temper may be better controlled because you are benefiting others.

> *Note*: Do **not** wear red, especially if you are angry, because your chances to attract accidents are maximized. By wearing red, your temper is brought out more. You are more impatient with others.

Red clothes or accessories should be worn if you are overly emotional or cry easily, dislike domesticity, have difficulties in the home or with women or the public. Also wear red if you are dictatorial, uncooperative with others or obsessed with taking measures which bring drastic changes.

The *Red* clothes or accessories may make you take action instead of crying over emotional upsets, frustrations or daily trifles. You may find it easier to take the initiative and pursue and accomplish worthwhile endeavors. You'll be more gutsy, energetic, aggressive and courageous. You may feel a strong urge to build an empire! Then you'll really be rich!

> *Note*: Do **not** wear green or you'll be counter-productive and bring out emotions and discordancy, which will hold you back from attracting wealth.

CHAPTER THREE
Sun Sign Wealth

Every sign of the zodiac has a potential for wealth; it depends upon whether you express the sign's positive or negative side.

ARIES... March 21 — April 19

You can attract wealth through being courageous, gutsy, competitive and a risk taker like Aries auto Racer Carl Yarborough. Or perhaps you may pioneer in new fields of endeavor like Aries born Hugh Hefner who started Playboy Clubs and a publishing empire. You may be a man of action like Arien Leonard Nimoy who not only is an actor but directs movies. As an Aries you do not take "no" for an answer. Speaking up didn't hurt Aries Howard Cosell's bank account. You fight for your beliefs like Aries Gloria Steinem who was involved in the women's lib movement. She is assertive and a real activist who tackled difficult tasks to make MS magazine a success.

Your fortune may come through being pushy, nervy and going where angels fear to tread like Arien Kitty Kelly who wasn't fearful when her life was threatened because of her exposé books. Riches can come when the strong urge overtakes you to conquer the world. You strive for personal leadership which can take you to the top. Be energetic like Aries born Diana Ross and use your enterprising nature to make your dreams come true. Let the idea of conquest stimulate you into doing enormous feats like Arien magician Harry Houdini. You must have freedom to follow the road of opportunity. Without a goal, you're restless.

If you want to be rich, avoid impatience, temper tantrums and big spending sprees. Don't let your gambling spirit make you lose your fortune at the casinos like Arien Omar Shariff. Watch impulsive action that leads down a road to nowhere. Stick to your chosen path or follow it until the end. Watch giving up when things get rough. Stay in for the long haul. Don't let impatience mess up your plans or quit a task at the first little setback. Concentrate energies on major accomplishments and don't get too bored with your new ideas and future plans. Don't leap into so many projects that you wind up abandoning most of them.

You get frustrated and irritable when you feel opportunity is passing you by and you haven't the money or freedom to pursue these chances. Try to be ready for them and when opportunities come, stop and think about what you really want. Force yourself to stop everything for a moment while you consider the pros and cons of all propositions. You need sense of balance and to think things through thoroughly before taking unnecessary chances, especially when high stakes are involved. Take time to listen to the advice of others. Don't use force on people because you want them to see things "your" way like Arien Joan Crawford when she ran Pepsi Cola or performed in movies. Avoid getting into hot water through telling it like it is. Diplomacy would help insure your success and bring prosperity.

TAURUS...April 20 — May 20

You can attract wealth through investing money wisely like Taurus born Queen Elizabeth II of England—her real estate holding alone are vast and mind blowing. The Queen's total assets are worth 9 billion dollars—she's the richest woman in the world. Or, perhaps you may be industrious and artistic like the actor and artist Taurean Anthony Quinn. Your riches may be gained through being thrifty and conservative like Taurean's Bing Crosby and Shirley Temple Black. The attitude of "If you spend money, you'll make money", has brought many Taureans great wealth. Your plodding effort is sure to make you a winner like Taurus born Barbara Streisand . Your finances could be in great shape through using your musical talent like Taurean's Stevie Wonder and Irving Berlin.

Taurus baseball great Willie Mays had unmistakable confidence that kept his bank account high. Taurus born Henry Fonda might have been slow in making decisions but his tranquil nature kept him in a wealthy bracket. Taureans like to collect art—Norton Simon is a good example of an affluent Taurean who did well along these lines. Strong-willed Taurean Cher has a blind determination that once she sets her mind on something—like exercise and bodybuilding—not even an earthquake will change her plans. Her persistence in planning a career, financial arrangements and trying to overcome her Chronic-Fatigue-Syndrome is admirable and typical of Taurus.

Like Taurean Aaron Spelling, a top and successful television producer who has spent millions on a mansion—your intense interest in acquiring an enormous fortune makes you plodding, careful, patient, and given to perfecting details. Your steadfast in mind and habit. No wonder you're a chinch to come out on top! People know they can depend on you like Taurean born Ella Fitzgerald who's always there to help at benefits for charity. Others trust your administrative skills, rely upon your efficiency and neatness. These traits have been expressed by Taurean Coretta Scott King, especially after her husband's assassination. These characteristics are aids to acquiring prosperity. Like Taurus born Katherine Hepburn, you are stable and seem to be similar to the Rock of Gibraltar. Your endurance, like boxer Taurus Sugar Ray Leonard, is just as great as your strength. Because you want a sure thing, you're like Taurus producer George Lucus, who doesn't take unnecessary risks.

If you want to be rich, learn to bend because if you're too stubborn you could lose out on some fabulous deals. Your downfall could be waiting too long for a project to mature—which was an admitted fault of Taurus Ryan O'Neal on a particular movie. Don't be so old-fashioned! Give the new and different a chance. Realize that, perhaps, there are better, quicker and more modern ways to perform tasks. You dislike changing those tried and sure methods for new ones because the old ways have worked for you in the past; however, this may not always hold true. Don't trample on people, or situations, like the Bull in the ring. You have difficulty dealing with people because you want your own way. You won't budge. Often this brings wealth, but at other times it distracts you from attaining the great riches that can be yours if you would just become a little more flexible.

GEMINI ... May 20 — June 20

You can attract wealth through the field of communication like Gemini, Joan Rivers, who is known for her glibness and sense of humor. Take a clue from the Geminian Henry Kissinger and cash in on your knowledge, ability to be fluent in many languages and to express your ideas readily. Or be like the wealthy Gemini comedian, Bob Hope, and capitalize on your wit. You are great at selling because not only do you have a great personality, but you can talk almost anyone into buying your wares; thus, you can use these attributes to get to the top. You can sell ideas or yourself to the public like Geminian ex-president George Bush.

You may want to make use of your great set of lungs and become rich and famous through vocalizing like Geminian singers Rosemary Clooney, Beverly Sills, Peggy Lee and Leslie

Uggams. Like Gemini Donald Trump, you are open minded and adaptable, thus, new fields are easy for you to enter and conquer. No wonder you can achieve success! Prosperity may be attracted through being versatile like Gemini actress-writer-designer, Joan Collins. Your intelligence can bring you wealth; thus, you need a profession that allows you to use your brains, such as famous lawyer, F. Lee Bailey. Financial security may come through making use of your multi-talents like Geminian Clint Eastwood who is an actor, director, mayor and restaurant owner. One thing sure about you is that you can always get a job.

If you want to be rich you should strive for stability. You should learn to stick to and perfect one thing. Changeableness is your downfall. Try to discipline yourself. Learn to concentrate on one important goal—like Gemini tennis champ Steffi Graf. Diversification is rewarding but first you must learn to focus your efforts on one important goal for success. Deliberately avoid known distractions. Learn to say "no." Curtail your social life and keep your nose to the grindstone. Riches can come if you make an effort to work hard and long hours. Party on weekends. During the week, tend to business. Don't burn your candle at both ends. Get your rest and direct your mental and physical energies into constructive career activities. Ride along on the ease with which you can do so many things. Avoid taking the risk of being a jack-of-all-trades. Prosperity may pass you by, if you waste time on unimportant things and overlook the big opportunities.

CANCER ... June 21 — July 22

You can attract wealth through following your hunches about what the public wants—just like Cancerian fashion designers Bill Blass, Pierre Cardan, Norma Kamalie and Oscar de la Renta. Your persistence and tenaciousness may pay off for you like it did for Cancerian actor-writer Sylvester Stallone, who didn't give up until his ROCKY movie script was produced. You're protective of those you work or deal with in business such as Cancerian born Bill Cosby who starred in a successful family TV show and was caring and nurturing toward the crew and cast members. No wonder your enterprises are booming! Prosperity may come to you if you are like Cancerian singers Lena Horne, Carley Simon, Jerry Vale and Barry Manilow and put feeling and emotion into your work. Your imagination and flair for the dramatic may bring you success through appearing on the stage and film, like Cancer Hume Cronyn or with writing like Cancer Barbara Cartland. You may be like the ice cream tycoon, Cancerian Tom Carvel, who became rich through food and Orville Redenbacher, the popcorn King. Your desire for variety may be satisfied by investing in many projects, thus, making you a multimillionaire like Cancerian Merv Griffin who owns hotels, casinos, produces game shows and has vast real estate holdings and so on.

If you want to be rich watch your emotions, moodiness and sensitivity. Avoid sulking and pouting—stay out of the shell you can so easily hide in. You can go so overboard in the preceding actions that you don't put your energy constructively into business or acquiring a fortune. Success may be difficult to attain if you are too touchy, changeable and don't assert yourself. Don't be afraid to take action because without action there's no movement. Possibly, you hold back from pursuing goals because you fear ridicule. You shouldn't worry about how others react to your behavior or activities. Instead you should realize that there are people who are kind, friendly, sympathetic and understanding. Those who don't fit into this category are not worth bothering about. Avoid becoming so discouraged, or your feelings so hurt, that you don't care about the job or business. Tend to your regular tasks. Visualize those happy moments in the past and ignore the current hurts. Don't shirk your responsibilities. Be tenacious as only you can be. To attain wealth, you must fight negativity, laziness and be gutsy, courageous and believe in yourself. Don't put all your energy into the easy way out—expecting that big win without hard work.

LEO ... July 23 — August 22

You can attract wealth through being an entrepreneur like Leo Born Adnan Khasoggi who is, allegedly very rich. He does everything in true Leo fashion, on a grand scale. A typical Leo trait is to delegate the actual work to top administrators which Leo born Giancarlo Giannini does—his wealth is enormous. Your affluence may come through leadership in the political arena like Leo born Menachem Began or industrial field tycoon Leonine Henry Ford. You have the ability to see the overview picture; thus, you don't get bogged down by detail. No wonder you're in demand.

'High expectations, and the persistence to follow through on ideas, can bring unlimited success—look at Leonine Carrol O'Conner who not only had a long running hit TV show but who owns a restaurant in Beverly Hills. Perhaps your prosperity comes from being on center stage like Leo singers Mick Jagger, Whitney Houston and Kenny Rodgers. The desire to be a star like Leo, Madonna, or in a high position like Leo Connie Chung could make you so ego driven that you become rich and famous. And like Madonna, you may continue to will yourself to work hard to achieve one goal after another.

Possibly, you're and overachiever like the late Leo born multimillionaire, Malcolm Forbes. Or perhaps you win lots of recognition and earn plenty of money like ex-sports celebrities, both Leo's, Frank Gifford and Leo Durocher. It's possible that the desire for respect, admiration, dignity, power and attention is so strong that you'll work hard to get to the top like Leonine Peter Jennings. You could swim your way to glory like Leo Esther Williams. Or, perhaps, cook your way to riches and fame like Leo born

Julia Child. Or, you may show off on the ice like Leonine's Dorothy Hamill and Peggy Fleming.

You should be proud of your achievements like Leo Neil Armstrong, the first man to walk on the moon. Success may come when you're a film director and enjoy telling stars how to act, such as Leo born Alfred Hitchcock. Or you want to be a producer like Leonine Norman Lear. You have the talent to be a good executive like Leo Lucille Ball, who also, was a great comedienne. Or do you want to shine like a star and gain wealth through acting talent, physical attributes and possessing a Lion's mane like Leonine Loni Anderson?

Success comes easily to you because you are fond of honors, awards and high office such as Leo Norman Schwarzkopf attained after the Desert Storm war. You crave to be in a position of authority which when attained, can help towards becoming affluent, such as, Jacqueline Kennedy Onassis—a true Leo, who became First Lady and very demanding when she gave orders at the White House. The climb up the ladder of success could be achieved through holding down many jobs and, in your spare time, running your own business. You possess great determination to rise to the top and your large ideas are grandly executed. You may run an empire like Leo born Napoleon Bonaparte, Emperor of France.

If you want to be rich, avoid being too egotistical, proud and dominating. Your thirst for glory could make you flaunt your ego and belittle others to the point that either they don't want to work for you or they do not want to be involved with you in business transactions. Avoid being overbearing or dictatorial in dealing with business associates and coworkers. You can get your way better and more, if you use the sugary approach of charming those with whom you deal. Guard against setting goals so enormous that you overshoot your mark. Curb extravagance. Try not to be so stubborn. It's difficult for you give in to others, but often it can payoff.

VIRGO ... August 23 — September 22

You can attract wealth through giving a service to others like Virgo born surgeon and specialist, Dr. Michael De Bakey. Prosperity may come if you are in a business that deals with facts, statistics and details. You may be a workaholic like Virgo born Geraldine Ferraro, or perhaps a perfectionist like Virgoan conductor Leonard Bernstein. Or, Perhaps you are neat, analytical and talented like singer-writer-dancer Michael Jackson — a real Virgo.

You are on the road to riches when you utilize your ability to find the flaws in other people's plans and discover the weaknesses in propositions and determine how they can be strengthened— something billionaire Billy Rose was able to do on a moment's notice. You are

46

always ready to suggest improvements and are able to see how the desired results can be obtained—Louis XVI, King of France used these Virgo traits when he built Versailles Palace.

Your approach is always earnest and sincere which Virgoan, Pia Lindstrom, expresses when she revues films and Broadway shows. Virgo born, Robin Leach, gained wealth through being flexible, mentally alert and taking an idea to show "The Lifestyles of the Rich and Famous" to the world. Financial security may come because you are practical, adaptable, serious, dependable, a contemplative thinker and take care of business as your first priority—billionaire Virgoan, John Kluge, one of the richest men in the U.S.A. is a perfect example of these Virgo characteristics.

If you want to be rich, avoid being too fussy and critical. Try to realize that no one's perfect; otherwise, your faultfinding could hold you back from attaining success. Avoid vacillating and putting things off, especially work you don't really want to do. Take charge of business. Stand up for your rights and beliefs. Speak out instead of keeping quiet. Voice those opinions in a diplomatic manner. Plan strategies and take action and you are sure to be a winner!

LIBRA ... September 23 — October 22

You can attract wealth through the arts like Libra born actress, Angela Lansbury. Or you may orchestrate all the different facets of yourself and keep them in balance and help others do the same such as Libran, Dr. Joyce Brothers. Or, perhaps you make your fortune through be musically creative and perform like actors-singers-writers both Librans, John Lennon and Anthony Newley. Or become a multimillionaire like Julio Iglesias—singing romantic songs on records in many languages that sell in enormous amounts worldwide. Prosperity may come if you dabble in many enterprises like my friend Mickey Rooney. He has so many businesses going at one time that it makes your head swim hearing about them! And that goes for Libran Gene Autry who owns a ball team and TV stations, among other assets.

Or your beauty may make you rich and famous like Libran models Cheryl Tiegs and Catherine Deneuve. Wealth may be attained through using your charming personality when you meet people personally or interview them like Libran Barbara Walters. If you socialize (a typical Libran activity) and come into contact with people who are beneficial to your career, you can be on top that much faster. Good fortune can come because you are helpful to others such as, Libran Jack La Lanne and his gyms. Usually when someone does you a favor, you are inclined to return it. Financial security may come because you're courteous, kind, fastidious, refined, neat and bright like Libran born Margaret Thatcher or a perfectionist like puppeteer, Libran Jim Henson. You don't like to hurt the feelings of others and like Libran Helen

Hayes, you are gracious and ever so considerate. No wonder you're successful! Your love of luxuries could give you your drive for affluence.

If you want to be rich you should learn how to say "no" to people; otherwise, you'll be spending most of your time attending parties which may be time consuming and may, or may not, help you accomplish your goals. Flattery is a weakness of yours, therefore, be leery of those who praise you constantly. Avoid extremes in trying to achieve the balance you crave. Try to make decisions. If you spend all of your time weighing the pros and cons, propositions and opportunities may be lost. Watch laziness.

SCORPIO ... October 23 — November 21

You can attract wealth through persistence, like Scorpio born Johnny Carson, regardless of the field of endeavor. You will stop at nothing to get what you want, such as Scorion Ted Turner. You are stubborn. You can get carried away by your wishes and strong intense desires. Ex-world champion, Scorpio born, Nadia Comaneci is an example of a person who didn't give up until she won. Like Scorpion born Robert F. Kennedy, you do not allow anyone or anything to stop you from reaching your goals. You must have total power and control. No wonder you're a success!

Perhaps you are like the Scorpio actress Kate Jackson who is a perfectionist at her work. You may have a great power of concentration like Scorpio born Marie Curie who co-discovered radium. Your desire to succeed is as intense as a burning fire. Take a lesson from Scorpion Marla Maples. This drive is so strong that at times you feel compelled to grapple with the most difficult and disagreeable tasks. Like Scorpio born Rev. Billy Graham, you've always got a plan to overcome obstacles. It's possible that you'll make a vast fortune because you are obsessed with work.

Perhaps you're rich because you are resourceful like Scorpio Roy Rogers who not only is a cowboy star but who has his name linked to fast food chains. Or you could be a multimillionaire like Scorpion Larry Flynt because you don't let opportunities pass by. Or, you may have an inexhaustible fund of ideas, like Scorpio born Roseanne, which can lead you , also, to the top. You are determined to be the best in your field like ex-tennis champion, and Scorpio born, Billie Jean King. Persistence, guts, courage and stick-to-itiveness are keys to success and these traits and actions when put into action could bring you the wealth you crave. Keen intuitive powers can guide you to riches; this insight didn't hurt Linda Evans or Whoopi Goldberg. Or, you may gain a fortune through being royalty, like Scorpio's King Hussein, Prince Charles, Princess Grace Kelly, and make wise financial investments

If you want to be rich, avoid being too forceful, dictatorial and sarcastic. Don't use underhanded methods to attack the competition. It's unnecessary because you are so dynamic that it is difficult for anyone to compete with you. Watch using the Scorpio sting when you don't get your own way. Realize that resentments hold you back from success. Your desire for control can make you lose many wonderful opportunities.

SAGITTARIUS...November 22—December 21

You can attract wealth through sales, investments, law, merchandising, counseling, shipping, exporting and importing. Or in the publishing field like Sagittarian Bob Guccione who owns Penthouse magazine. It's possible you'll make a fortune in sports like these Sagittarians: baseball players Joe DiMaggio and George Foster; champion gymnast Cathy Rigby; champion skier Suzy Chaffee, tennis champion Chris Everet; golfer Lee Trevino. Or perhaps, like Sagittarian born Jane Fonda who made— and still is making—millions of dollars on her exercise-workout videos as well as her movies. You are very decided about what you want like Sagittarius billionaire J. Paul Getty who waited for twenty years so he could buy out share holders of Getty Oil.

Prosperity may come because you think big like Sagittarian Walt Disney who not only initiated animated cartoons but conceived Disneyland—largest amusement park in the world. Disneyland expanded to foreign countries (Japan, France), typical of Sagittarius who is known as the sign with wanderlust. Or you are confident, positive, decisive, self-reliant, enthusiastic and talented like Frank Sinatra and Mary Martin. Perhaps, you are ambitious of worldly position like Sagittarian Winston Churchill. This drive can take you to the top and be financially rewarding. Perhaps your extreme wealth comes through talent combined with optimism, and being adaptable, flexible, cheerful, friendly, outgoing, trusting, honest, jovial and having a good sense of humor such as Sagittarians Ossie Davis and Dick Clark.

You may get rich and famous through comedy like these Sagittarians: Harpo Marx, Howie Mandell, Richard Pryor, Wally Cox, Woody Allen, Flip Wilson, Redd Foxx, Rodney Dangerfield and that zany performer Bette Midler whose antics took her to the top quickly. Success is easily attained because you believe that "Everything happens for the best," and "There's a reason for everything;" thus, you don't let things get you down. Sagittarian Robin Givens must have had this attitude when she went through her trying ordeal with ex-husband Mike Tyson. She came through it with typical Sagittarian flying colors and has become a better than ever performer.

You are visionary and can see wealth coming toward you like Sagittarius producer of films—Steven Spielberg and opera star Maria Callas (a Sagittarian too) and that ever so clever writer, Noel Coward (another Sagittarian). There are many wealthy Sagittarians such as Aga Khan who was worth his weight in gold (putting on pounds is something Sagittarians have to fight more than other zodiac signs) and those who were born into wealth—Christina Onassis, Doris Duke, Dina Merrill and Cornelia Guest.

If you want to be rich avoid restlessness, overspending, expanding too rapidly without having first thought things thoroughly through. Guard against making impulsive decisions. You learn by your mistakes, and later can profit from them. However, you don't let your errors disturb you. Your attitude is, "That's life!" You need to be more disciplined and discreet. You tend to burn up your vitality through over-intensity which can often hinder success.

Your bluntness can cause problems with others and, thus, you may lose important deals. You need to learn diplomacy. Also it's important for you to carefully aim your goals (The famous Sagittarian arrow may miss the mark if you haphazardly approach things.) You will need to work hard for success and wealth, so avoid "goofing off" in playland.

CAPRICORN...December 22—January 19

You can attract wealth through being industrious and responsible like Capricorn multimillionaire Thierry Roussell who manages the family fortune or like Capricorns Jean Stapleton and Mary Tyler Moore who for years stuck with their hit television series. Perhaps you are like Capricorn born Dolly Parton whose ambition and persistence took her to the top. Not only is she a singer and actress, but owns her Dollywood Theme Park. She planned (a typical Capricorn trait) her publicity campaign five years ahead so she would be famous.

Muhammad Ali, a Capricorn, worked hard in training and became the world's boxing champion. Success can come because you are able to climb around the obstacles thrown in your path like former Capricorn, F.B.I. Chief, J. Edgar Hoover. Your "one-step-at-a-time" attitude can take you to the top. It didn't hurt Capricorn Conrad Hilton when he formed the Hilton chain of hotels. You can wait patiently for your plans to mature just like Capricorn Richard Nixon did for years when he continued in his bid for the Presidential position at the White House. His take charge personality came beaming through.

You are clever, an excellent organizer and excel in management such as Capricorn Georgette Mosbacher who made a fortune when she sold her La Prarie skin care and cosmetics firm. You have a wonderful know-how when it comes to economizing. Prosperity may come because you are diplomatic, and have the ability to maneuver others with skill like Capricorn born Aristotle Onassis and Grant Tinker. No wonder it's in your stars that you can, when you apply yourself, be extremely wealthy!

You are cautious, systematic, serious and a good reasoner like Capricorn best-selling author Judith Krantz. Like Capricorn's Charo and Cary Grant, you can grasp every opportunity to get to the top. Your drive to go after worldly success, money and high position makes you a real winner like singers Elvis Presley, Rod Stewart—both Capricornian's. You can be stubborn as the mountain goat ruled by your sign. The late Howard Hughes, a multimillion-aire Capricorn, stuck to his guns and refused to budge until he was in complete control of TWA—buying up shares quicker than you could shake a stick.

If you want to be rich, avoid being pessimistic. Your negative thoughts could hold your back from attaining those status positions you dream about. You must take care that you are not your own worst enemy, especially, when you refuse to change and adapt to others. You won't bend to anyone. Your desire for power can get you into hot water, if it is misused; especially, if you take advantage of others by finding their weak points and lording it over them until they do your bidding. You won't give an inch until you get your way.

You can often be a miser and not want to share with others. A "Sharing the wealth" policy enables you to build your assets into an empire. Guard against selfishness. Capricorn greed can be your downfall. If you use others, remember, "What goes around, comes around."

Watch wallowing in self-pity. When you feel sorry for yourself, you cut off opportunities to attract money. Realize that others do appreciate all of your sacrifices, and those who don't, are not worth wasting your precious time on them. You need to stop complaining. When you gripe and are suspicious of others, you hold back your earning power because your associates don't want to deal with that type of negativity. Try to smile once in a while.

Your are guided through stormy waters. You are a survivor! Put long-range gains before short-range ones. You are easily disciplined. Your pride, ambition and deliberation makes you accomplish your goals. You earn your wealth through hard and laborious work. You don't allow setbacks to deter you from accomplishing your plans to go all the way to the top—honors, high offices and affluence.

AQUARIUS...January 20—February 18

You can attract wealth through inventions like Aquarian Thomas Edison (Electricity is ruled by the sign Aquarius.) Your Aquarian riches could come through new products such as actor Paul Newman's salad dressings. He donates this money to charity (A typical humanitarian action which is representative of the sign Aquarius.) You could make money from crusades the way Aquarians Betty Friedan and Susan B. Anthony (leading figures in the women's movements)—book sales helped Miss Friedan on TV.

You could make your fortune through promoting yourself and your jewelry designs such as Aquarian Vanna White. You may be artistic and creative like Aquarian Suzanne

Pleshette who designed linens. Your daring to be different could have mass appeal that could wind up making you rich. It didn't hurt Tallulah Bankhead. Or you may become super rich like Aquarian talk show hosts Oprah Winfrey and Arsenio Hall. Or acting and being witty could get you to the top like it did with Aquarian's George Burns and Zsa Zsa Gabor.

Prosperity may come because you are friendly, sincere, persistent, and interested in political issues such as Aquarian's Ted Koppel, and ex-president's Abraham Lincoln, Franklin D. Roosevelt and Ronald Reagan. You are intuitive, progressive and interested in new discoveries. Your originality, unusual ideas, innovative and untried courses of action appeal to you and can make you a fortune such as with Aquarians Mia Farrow, Yoko Ono and Charles Lindberg.

Your magnetism and acting ability could be assets that could make you affluent like Aquarians Lana Turner and Clark Gable. You know how to talk to the public , and individuals on a one-to-one basis. These private chit-chat sessions show your talent to tune into individuals so they'll react to your words kindly and go along with your beliefs. Aquarian Oral Roberts is able to do this with the masses on television when he appeals for huge sums of money to help support his shows and other projects. By applying your energies, constructively, you can reap a bundle of money.

If you want to be rich, avoid getting so carried away with your humanitarian interests that you don't tend to business. When you spend most of your time gadding about and goofing off with your numerous friends, you'll be distracted from work. Thus, under these circumstances, it's difficult for you to acquire a fortune. You are unpredictable which could cause losses. When you are unreliable it hinders your success. Therefore, tend to be more punctual and dependable. Try to avoid being abrupt; it hurts the feelings of others, although you don't do it intentionally. Your "I-know-it-all" attitude can hinder you from learning about new products, courses to take or ideas that could make you rich. Try to keep an open mind and give other's a chance to express themselves. You could learn something new, and prosperity could follow.

PISCES ... February 19—March 20

Like Rupert Murdock, a Piscean who acquired wealth through the publishing empire he built, you can wheel and deal. Or your wise investments, TV commercials and shows all aid to make you rich such as Piscean born Ed McMahon. Prosperity may be attracted through your beauty, if you model like Ivana Trump—a Piscean who started at that rung of the ladder only to move upward when she married wealth and ran the Plaza Hotel in NYC. She promotes her products and various talents. Promoting is a typical Piscean occupation, and public relations is one of Piscean Stedman Graham's enterprises.

You may acquire prosperity through selling your perfumes, like Piscean beauty Elizabeth Taylor—Passion and Diamonds are increasing her wealth by millions of dollars—perhaps, even billions! Why not get rich as an actress? Be like Piscean Glenn Close—talented, versatile and adaptable. She is able to pretend and make believable a variety of roles. Or Piscean Rob Reiner who is a great actor, writer, director and producer and finds it easy to perform these various job-related occupations.

Increase your bank account by using your imagination and love of mystery to write detective stories like Piscean Mickey Spillane. Or you may become rich through being like Pisces born Patricia Nixon who was self-sacrificing so her husband could become President and run the U.S.A. Be a designer like multimillionairess Gloria Vanderbilt—a Piscean. Express your creativity like Pisces actor-writer-producer of music(records) and TV show—Jackie Gleason. Or use your talented voice by dramatizing various roles in animated movies like Pisces Jim Backus.

Be poetical like Piscean born Elizabeth Barrett Browning. Increase your finances by being versatile like Piscean Dinah Shore who made plenty from combined assets—cooking, singing, acting, and golf. Her kindness and warmth embodied the wonderful Pisces traits. You can be at the top of almost any line of endeavor as varied as Harry Karl and his shoe industry before he gambled it away (a bad Piscean trait that can ruin you). By the way Harry Karl was a Piscean and shoes are a Piscean occupation since the feet are represented by the sign Pisces. Or to another extreme, be father of your country like Piscean George Washington. Or go into a recording career like Piscean Johnny Cash; a vocation that can make you millions of bucks, if you don't get cheated out of royalty payments. (Note: The discordant side of Pisces is cheating or being cheated.)

Turn your natural assets into money-making ventures and become affluent. However, don't magnify or blow things out of proportion. Often your downfall stems from believing too much in the schemes of others. You can be gullible and easily deceived—and there goes your money!

Don't make promises that you can't keep; otherwise, other's will avoid doing business with you. Live on a schedule, thus, avoiding procrastination. Try not to give in to a lazy streak. If you sit around drifting and dreaming, you'll be held back from a top spot. To succeed, you must replace inaction with action because without movement there's nothing. Try to finish projects started so you can gain the prosperity you yearn for. Don't lie. You'll be caught and word will get out that you are not to be trusted... and that's no way to cash in on millions!

CHAPTER FOUR
Relationships

Do you know that the people you are in contact with through business or in your personal life could hinder your financial success? The negativity of a mate, loved one, relative, friend, partner, boss or employee could wear off on you. You could be industrious and talented but may wonder, "What am I doing wrong? Why have I failed to get to the top?" Perhaps you are not aware that the real reason you did not live up to your expectations was due to your relationships.

A negative person may be described as insecure, easily depressed, fearful, suspicious, envious, angry, resentful or one who complains constantly. He/she is inclined to cry the blues, be narrow-minded and selfish. It is difficult for you to be wealthy if you are in daily contact with this type of individual.

J.D. is a Realtor and client of mine. His booming business started to go sour a few months after his marriage. Once deals started falling through, he cut down on personal expenses. At that moment his wife became insecure and started to feed him negative energy in daily doses. She would say, "You'll never amount to anything again. You don't have that certain something to stay on top. You're a failure. You don't know how to handle clients.

You don't know how to run a business successfully. You are a weakling." The more she did this, the more business declined. After a year she divorced him and married a wealthy man. The moment they separated his business improved and by the time the divorce came through his earnings and investments added up to a sizable sum. That was twenty years ago and today he is doing a thriving business and is happily married for twelve years to a woman who gives him daily doses of laughter, confidence and encouragement—all the ingredients one needs to be rich—and he is!

If you are not happy in your home or working environment, it is difficult to attract success. If you are in daily contact with a mate, loved one, relative, friend, partner, boss or employee and this individual believes in you and encourages you to go out and "conquer the world"—this person is in your corner 100% and gives you such a "high" that you will do everything in your power to either reach, or stay, at the top. Your spirits are lifted with such enthusiasm that it's easy to attract money.

There is nothing worse than spending so many hours a day in misery just because you dislike the boss or a coworker or have difficulty with an employee or client. It's not good to engender hatred by being nasty, cold, sarcastic, and unsympathetic toward others. This detracts from business success and brings about a loss of money, employment and even ill health. If you own or run a large corporation this could also result in a mass turnover of employees, causing a slowdown in production and earning the company a bad reputation, especially with personnel recruiting agencies.

People tend to like you when you are nice, kind, gracious, friendly, and understanding. A smile goes a long way to brighten up even the most dismal rainy day. Spreading good cheer sends out harmony that will bounce right back to you, the sender.

When you give your trust it's usually returned, although there are exceptions to this depending upon the other person's Sun sign and your compatibility with him/her. When you distrust someone, that individual feels it. This never encourages good business or working relationships, though it's wise to be cautious, and not a fool. By knowing all about a person's zodiac sign, you will discover whether you have to be on guard so you are not taken advantage of.

Often you cannot ask a boss his/her Sun sign; however, there are give-away traits that clue you in to whether a person is the negative or positive type. Usually the negative type is an individual who is thin, bony, or heavy set, serious, grim, seldom smiles and gripes and complains constantly. Usually the positive type is heavy-set, jolly, outgoing, pleasant, friendly and is always smiling and seems to make the best of all situations. These are both generalities, however most of the time they fit. As you know the famous adage, "Birds of a feather, flock together," or "like attracts like." So, it's possible that there is something negative within you that draws a pessimist into your life. Or your positive traits draws an optimist into your life.

A brief description of Sun signs who are compatible with each other follows: *Aries* with *Taurus, Gemini, Leo, Libra, Sagittarius, Aquarius* and *Pisces*. *Taurus* with *Aries, Gemini, Cancer, Virgo, Libra, Scorpio, Capricorn* and *Pisces*. *Gemini* with *Aries, Taurus, Cancer, Leo, Libra, Sagittarius* and *Aquarius*. *Cancer* with *Taurus, Gemini, Leo, Virgo, Scorpio, Capricorn* and *Pisces*. *Leo* with *Aries, Gemini, Cancer, Virgo, Libra, Sagittarius, Aquarius* and *Pisces*. *Virgo* with *Taurus, Cancer, Leo, Libra, Scorpio, Capricorn* and *Pisces*. *Libra* with *Aries, Taurus, Gemini, Leo, Virgo, Scorpio, Sagittarius, Aquarius* and *Pisces*. *Scorpio* with *Taurus, Cancer, Virgo, Libra, Sagittarius, Capricorn* and *Pisces*. *Sagittarius* with *Aries, Gemini, Leo, Libra, Scorpio, Capricorn* and *Aquarius*. *Capricorn* with *Taurus, Cancer, Virgo, Scorpio, Sagittarius, Aquarius* and *Pisces*. *Aquarius* with *Aries, Gemini, Leo, Libra, Sagittarius, Capricorn* and *Pisces*. *Pisces* with *Aries, Taurus, Cancer, Leo, Virgo, Libra, Scorpio, Capricorn* and *Aquarius*.

Often the same Sun signs are compatible with each other, however this does not always hold true—each individual horoscope compared to one another is the best way to ascertain compatibility. If the Sun signs are not compatible there could be other planets between the two horoscopes that are compatible; therefore, Sun sign compatibility by itself is not the complete answer, but it is a big help.

Are you aware that when you hire employees who are compatible with you, their Sun signs should also blend with one another? And when the entire company is in symmetry, prosperity is much easier to achieve!

The cliché, "It takes two to tango (tangle)," describes perfectly how each individual is responsible for his/her behavior and that one person alone is not the culprit. If you understand one another and try to control destructive tendencies so everyone can benefit, you are well on your way to the road to the top.

Avoid negative influences and people who tend to pull you down. How do you deal with them if you must be around them? It is not easy especially if it's a loved one; however, if you think it is worth the effort, give it a whirl. If you must be surrounded by those who are critical or gripe and complain—stay out of their way as much as possible and don't internalize the abuse; keep in mind, it is the other person's problem. Try to be around those who stimulate, inspire and encourage you to do your best--the enthusiastic type of personality.

Eventually you may tire of consuming so much time and energy on trying to keep your mate in a positive frame of mind. Often negativity is expressed only during specific time periods(when there's an aspect in the horoscope which could be in for a year, month, or for years), although some people seem to be born with it. If the former is the case, you are both lucky because it won't last; if the latter be the case, you may want to do some rethinking about the relationship.

If a friend, relative, loved one or mate says, "You'll never have a dime or be successful, "let this be a challenge. Take action and prove that you are misjudged. However don't discuss it any further and keep your projects a secret until they are successful. If this method doesn't appeal to you, it may be in your best interest to end the relationship or stay away from the person, especially if your financial condition has worsened.

If someone says, "Times are bad. The economy is the pits. I can't see anything improving. Bad luck is everywhere"—you can either ignore these thoughts by blocking them out and replacing them with harmonious ones or you may kindly and firmly answer, "My business is great. Most of the people I know are happy and successful. Please don't send out negative thoughts to me because I know that my good is everywhere and I am going to be okay."

If you are in a partnership, perhaps your associate is holding you back from expansion due to a fear of spending money. This could be detrimental to the success of your enterprise.

Often a discussion with a third party, i.e., an accountant, may help. Negative people think small; positive people think big. You attract what you think!

If you believe your boss is holding you back from advancing, change your job or your attitude. Tell yourself, "My boss thinks very highly of me and the way I perform my duties. I appreciate this heavy work load because it is an indicator that he knows I can handle it."(Often in the beginning when you talk to yourself you may have to lie until it becomes a reality.) If things don't change after a while then realize that it is time for you to make a move and go on to better things. You'll be right if you continue to tell yourself, "I will never get a salary increase from this miser!" The thoughts you send bounce back and then it makes it more difficult to get a raise. Your financial condition is likely to improve much faster when you change your negative thoughts to positive ones.

Generally a negative person is selfish and only thinks about how things affect him/her. If you refuse to listen to negative words of a loved one, you could be given the silent treatment which could worsen things between you. Discordant thoughts gives the other person power over you. You are placing limitations upon yourself. It's as if you are a prisoner to this bad situation which you have created for yourself. You may feel helpless and think that there's no hope for anything better. To help relieve yourself of this type of thinking, repeat to yourself, "I am fearless and know that the creator(or God) loves and protects me."

Negative energy is a strong and destructive force which can hold you back from your goals. The more dislike or hate that is sent out, the more is returned to the sender. Therefore, send out thoughts of love(it may be impersonal love rather than "romantic") to others. Thoughts produce things; thus, relationships should improve, and material gains can be more easily attracted. And that is what it's all about, isn't it?

If you want to continue a relationship or are thrown into contact with a negative person, it is best to protect yourself. Imagine a screen or glass cage around you with a hole in the top for air. Visualize the other person on the outside unable to penetrate, touch or harm you.

Another strategy you may find useful is to look for the good traits in others and compliment them at every possible moment. Flattery boosts the ego, increases the vitality, helps win friends and influence the right people, as well as it endears you to the receiver. A few suggested sentences you may want to use are:"You sure are a hard worker." "Your ideas are ingenious." "Your business plans are wonderful." "I am so proud of you." "You look great in that outfit." "Your tie is attractive." I like your shirt(dress, sweater, etc.)." "You have good taste."

It is always best to bless others, wish them well and try to picture them as positive, happy, rich and successful. If you picture others as failures, you'll be sending out negative pictures which could come bouncing back to you. Then you may wonder, "How did I fail?" Therefore a "money magic" secret with relationships is to picture and think of, everyone as wealthy, content, and successful.

When you praise and bless others, you can do it mentally rather than orally. These actions are like irresistible magnets that connects your vibrations to the other individual's and comes bouncing back to you. It may take a while for people to respond to your praises. Not only can you bless people but you can bless your job, the stores you go to, the air you breathe, the world and everything in your vicinity. Send out thoughts of love and thank God, the Creator, for all the good you have. Be grateful for your material blessings, for the people in your life and anything else you can think of.

Be understanding. Be tolerant of the views and shortcomings of others. Realize that no one is perfect. Send out positive mental energy which is a strong invisible command that taps the higher sources such as God, the Creator. This energy flows into the subconscious of the other person and it is the divine spark within you .

Also you can say, "To all those who come into contact with me, you will receive love and prosperity." When you praise a person for the qualities he/she lacks, suddenly those traits can become a part of his/her personality. Instead of getting angry and fighting, tune in to the individual's good traits. Ignore the bad characteristics as if they don't exist—and then maybe they won't exist. If the person is irresponsible, send him thoughts that he will be responsible. Hold the thought clear in your mind and then release it. Visualize what you want to see. Look at this individual with warm, tender and loving feelings. Expect only good for them. Believe that the divine spark within you is going to help you and those you contact mentally or physically. Tell yourself, "I unite with this positive energy which will bring perfect results and happiness. I praise the world, the goodness in it for me....for you...for everyone. I bless others and send out thoughts of love to the world."

Money Magic means positive thinking, not only in relation to yourself but also concerning others. *Thoughts Produce Things*: therefore, always think positive and then you'll be on your way to make your dreams come true.

CHAPTER FIVE
Money and Negative Thinking

Are you aware of the fact that you may be guilty of negative thinking on a daily basis? The majority of people do not realize that certain expressions are negative. The adage, "You attract what you think" is a very true statement. Thoughts DO produce things; therefore what you tell yourself, you will attract.

If you are not careful with your thinking, you just may attract something you really don't want. Therefore, try to analyze a thought as to what it really implies. If you discover it is negative, reword the sentence so it will be positive thus bringing you the things you really desire.

Do you know that the word "hope" is negative? The word "hope" means that you hope it will happen but you are **not** sure it will. This is a form of doubting, such as, "I hope that I'll have good luck and win the lottery." Instead of using the word "hope," replace it with "know," i.e., "I know this is going to happen." "I know that I'm a winner.""I know" is stronger than "I hope." "I know" means that **You Are Sure** you are going to get what you want; thus, enhancing your chances of having your dreams fulfilled. Often a person may say, "I don't have any money," or "I don't have the money to buy—," or "I can't afford—." Avoid making these statements even if you believe they are true. If you say, "I don't have any money, " you'll be right because you just told yourself that, and you may continue not to have any money until you change your thinking. If you say, "I can't afford—," you're right; you can't afford it because you just told yourself so, and that makes it a reality. Instead say, "I don't want to spend the money I have on—." This implies that *you have* the money but just don't want to spend it at this time on that particular object or whim. As a result you will continue to have and attract money.

Do you have a poverty consciousness? Do you think that you'll never have much money? Are you guilty of saying any of the following? "I'll never have any money because I'm not qualified to earn a lot," or "I'll never be rich because I'm not lucky enough to win or inherit wealth," or "I am poor." If you see yourself as poor, you are right and will continue to be poor until you get rid of your poverty consciousness by replacing it with money consciousness. You are correct that you're not lucky if you say, "I am not lucky." And you will continue to be unlucky until you reprogram your mind. If you say, "I'm not qualified to earn a lot of money" perhaps you are speaking the truth. If this be the case, do something about it. Take a special course, learn a new field and in the interim you may have to sacrifice some fun, friends, love and money. However, think about the day when you'll be rewarded with earning big bucks!

The mind can **not** think a positive and negative thought at the same time and get **one** result. You can't say, "I am going to get this job," and then a few hours later say, "I don't think I will get that job." Most of the time a negative thought is stronger than a positive one. Therefore say, "I am going to get the job that is right for me." Thus, you'll release the energy so you will get a job that is great for you.

Never say, "I am saving money for a rainy day," because that statement sends out the negative thought that you are **not** going to have money in the future and that is why **now** you are saving it. You are doubting that you will be financially secure at some later date. If you continue to think this way, you'll attract the rainy day.

Try to avoid saying, "When I get paid next week, I am going to buy —." "When I sell this house I am going to spend my commission on a trip around the world," "I'm expecting a refund on my taxes from IRS and when it arrives I am going to treat myself to a mink coat," "When I win this lawsuit, I am going to buy a boat." The preceding sentences are examples of how you can mentally spend money before you actually receive it. This type of thought stops the flow of money that should be coming to you. As a result, usually some emergency occurs and you are unable to spend the money as planned.

Do you ask psychics or astrologers, "Am I going to get this money?" or "Will I be rich?" If you ask these questions then you are doubting that you are going to get the money or be rich. One doubt can negate everything good that is working on your behalf. Instead ask, "When am I going to get this money?" or better still you should tell yourself, "I know I am going to get this money, therefore I am not going to think about it anymore. I will release the energy so it will happen."

Another form of negativity is the individual who places limits, or restricts himself by making up excuses: "I can't do this." Or "I can't get a job." Or "I didn't get the breaks." Or my education isn't good enough for me to compete." Or " If I had been born rich, I could make a fortune like the other wealthy children." Or "It's all a matter of luck and it's not coming in my direction." Or "If I was given a chance, I could get to the top." Or "It's this desk work that holds me back from advancing."

It's easy to get in a rut when you limit yourself with these excuses because if you really wanted to do something, you would. However because it's not in your heart to do a particular thing, or you are too lazy to earn money through hard work, you make up alibis and limit yourself. If you really wanted a job, there's plenty of work out there such as stuffing envelopes, delivery or messenger occupations. However, the jobs that are available may not pay the salary you want, and need, or they may be beneath you or you may be unqualified for them. Therefore don't limit yourself by saying you can't get a job. If you continue this type of thinking, you'll be on the unemployment list until you change your thoughts.

Thoughts of failure are negative. Often famous people think they are going to fail once they reach the top. Others don't even attempt to be successful because they can't stand the thought of failure once they've made it big. Greta Garbo thought along these lines. This type of thinking is based upon insecurity. The horoscope of Adolph Hitler indicated that he had these failure thoughts. The thing he feared came to pass, thus, proving that "You attract what you think." Often a person is afraid to make sacrifices to secure a high position. Usually when you want to be rich you have to pay the piper and make sacrifices along the way, unless you are lucky and win at gambling or inherit wealth.

Perhaps you are in business for yourself and are afraid of expanding. Fearing that you won't do well, or should not take the chance, are ways of expressing negativity. Never expand a business when you send out these types of thoughts because this is "loss" energy and losses are then easily attracted. If you do go against your thinking and expand, less and less money may come in and you may wind up either going out of business or renting a smaller and less expensive place. If this occurs, usually losses are attracted because your mind has stopped growing for the bigger things. The more worried you become, the more financial problems you attract. If you raise your prices when you are in a negative mental condition, a loss could occur. Change your thinking if you want your business and, thus, money to increase.

Have you noticed that when you started to pinch pennies your financial problems increased? And the tighter money became, the more frugal you became? Then you may have lost a job or had emergencies that took most of your meager savings. You may have thought, "The money has just stopped coming." It isn't the money that stopped, because there's always cash out there for you to win or earn. It is *YOUR* **mind that stopped thinking positive thoughts**, thus, causing you difficulties. When you cut down on the spending almost to the point of being a miser, your subconscious mind is saying, "I'd better start to save money or I won't have any." When you deny yourself material possessions and food because you are afraid to spend the money you have, your subconscious mind is likely to feel the sacrifice. When that panic button gets hit, you become gravely concerned for the future. Depression and self-pity soon follow.

When you hoard money it is difficult, although not impossible, to attract it. Often a person who becomes rich also becomes a miser, because subconsciously he doesn't have the confidence that he will continue to have money. The loved ones or bad investments could cost him dearly, and that is the start of his going to the extreme with frugality. The more he hoards, the more he worries he'll lose what he has. This negativity could be, eventually, damaging to his bank account and could start his financial decline.

You've read about the poorly dressed old lady who lived and died in poverty and yet had lots of money hidden under the mattress? This type of person's negativity is in not trusting the bank with her savings. She may have deprived herself of clothes, a refrigerator, fun, food, etc., in order to hoard the money. Then upon her death, the relatives inherit and spend it. Deprivation is a form of negative thinking. The individual, subconsciously, believes she won't have any money if she doesn't sacrifice and go without things. Usually she is the type who is lonely, reclusive, easily depressed, feels sorry for herself and that this is her lot in life.

Another type of negative person is the one who, continually, complains, "Why does everything bad happen to me?" "I can't do anything right." "Times are hard." "The economy is getting worse every day." "There's nothing out there for me." The more she believes it, the more for her it will come true. If you listen to the problems, tragedies and worries of others, you'll temporarily tune in to the same negative energy; thus, if you are the type of person to absorb it to the point you take on the same mental outlook, it won't be long until you start to repel, instead of attract, money. Also if you watch sad television shows, movies or worry about the latest news report, you are tuning in to negative energy--it's like a vicious circle that keeps going round and round. And once you are caught up in it, it's hard to break loose.

When you are extremely emotional and negative and burden your troubles on another, you not only feel worse by reliving it but you give the other person a huge dose of doom and gloom. People flee from this because they have enough problems of their own. However, while listening to you, they may be worn down to a frazzle and drained of energy. If you do this on a regular basis to your pals, you are a mental parasite stealing the positive energy of your listener. Then, do you wonder why you are lonely? Or, why you don't have many friends? When you saturate others with your upsets and frustrations, it becomes difficult to attract wealth.

Another form of negativity is the cry baby who is so emotional that the wrong tone of voice or look makes her unload a bucketful of tears. She may have difficulty in becoming prosperous.

The gossip who spreads the latest juicy story or who talks about everyone all the time is expressing negative energy. It will be difficult for her to increase her finances because being a tattletale lowers the vibratory rate and, thus, problems are soon encountered.

You could be held back from acquiring the riches you long for when you are resentful, envious or jealous. Success is difficult to attain when you envy the possessions, prosperity and good luck of another person. *Envy* is discontent because someone else is in the position you believe you should be in; it is a feeling that makes you begrudge another his good fortune. *Resentment* is a deep sense of injury and anger arising from a sense of wrong, i.e., you resent the individual who got the promotion you thought you deserved. Therefore, you are strongly displeased because you didn't get what you feel is yours. *Jealousy* stems from suspicious fears. Perhaps you are jealous because a friend seems to have more advantages than you.

Often a person may hold negative thoughts which work against you, without you or the individual realizing it. For example, you may tell a pal about a job that you think you are going to get. She may respond with, 'I think that it will be a wonderful break for you. I'm so glad for you." However, subconsciously she is thinking, "She's not going to get that job because she didn't get the last one she was interviewed for." Perhaps, a few of your other friends' reactions are the same. Then it isn't long until you've suddenly got a mass of negative energy bombarding your subconscious mind. And the next thing you know, you are telling yourself, "I'm not going to get that job." Therefore, be secretive about interviews, auditions, projects, investments, contests, gambling, financial transactions, etc., because you never know who might innocently send you negative thoughts(energy). When this energy is sent in your direction it makes it difficult to attain your goals. The best thing to do is surprise your chums with the good news after you've received the job, money or won the lottery.

If you talk too much about a project, you expend the energy thus making it difficult to accomplish. For example, perhaps, you have a fantastic idea to write a book. After you've written a few chapters you start calling all your friends to read excerpts from it. You consume so much time talking about it on the telephone that either you don't have the time to finish it, or you bore of it and abandon it in midstream. Naturally, this is not how success or riches are attained.

Other losses are attracted when your mind is up in the clouds. Perhaps you are in a business that involves wheeling and dealing. Projects may start to fall through. A client doesn't keep his promises. Your heart is set on this venture and you are sure it's going to make you rich overnight. It's possible that you put too much faith on another person's word and, thus, **limited** *yourself* because you didn't approach anyone else for this project. Perhaps you were too lazy to see about other possibilities, or just believed too much in the credibility of the other party. Then when you are left holding the bag, you wonder, "What happened? What did I do wrong?" Limitations, laziness, overconfidence in another's word, being unrealistic and becoming involved in get rich-quick schemes are all negative actions which detract from the attainment of prosperity.

Do you think that someone is blocking you from an important position, raise, award, vote, etc.? If somebody is, perhaps you should reevaluate your job or the situation and make a change for the better. Or is it nothing more than your ego getting in the way? Perhaps, you feel that you are better than your co-workers, therefore, you should be the one promoted. Possibly, the boss does not agree with you, hence you feel he is the obstacle to your success. Your employer could dislike the way you handle others, i.e., lording it over them, being bossy, arrogant and bragging about your capabilities. Perhaps, you treat the coworkers like they are beneath you. It is important to have a strong ego drive if you want to be rich and at the top; however, if you behave in the manner as just mentioned, you could be held back from the glory and prosperity you crave and then you would really be miserable.

CHAPTER SIX
How to Attract Money and Success

Everyone has a dream. It's what picks you up and gives you energy. Perhaps you dream of wealth, success, love and happiness. Do you know that *Within You* is the power to make *your* dreams come true? Thoughts produce things, thus thoughts which attract wealth have the power to bring you all of the money, homes, yachts, furs, jewels, and so on, that you want. However negative thoughts can deny those very things you yearn to possess.

All affluent people have started out with a conviction of their prosperity and then have followed their inner feelings until they have accomplished their goal. These individuals have always possessed a single thought—success! They knew what they wanted and went after it. Also along the way they made valuable contacts with their fellow man. They knew how to win friends and influence others in business deals.

Success makes you feel that others respect you. It builds your ego so that you expect a lot from others. Perhaps you expect to be catered to in restaurants—getting better service. But to gain prosperity you must have a certain amount of knowledge—knowledge of your profession, how to get along with those you work or deal with—and you must have a definite aim and choose the course of action to get that goal.

Stick to it regardless of the obstacles placed in your pathway. Adapt to the changing environment in business; keep up with the times.

Don't be afraid to go after what you want. Avoid getting your mind bogged down by negative emotions and limitations. The Fixed signs of the zodiac—Taurus, Leo, Scorpio and Aquarius--have to learn to be open to new ideas and not close the door to them. Tap the source to bring the riches and new avenues of profit will be there for you to grasp. Closed minds bring closed doors. The Adaptable signs of the zodiac—Gemini, Virgo, Sagittarius and Pisces —are able to make quick changes and flexible for new areas of gain; thus, it's easy for success to follow. The Action signs of the zodiac— Aries, Cancer, Libra and Capricorn—are able to get things moving but have to watch losing interest in midstream. But these *action* signs are the idea people; the *fixed* signs can perfect and persistently stick to these ideas to make them successful; the *adaptable* signs can tell the world about them.

Climb to the higher levels you desire; if you fall a little, get up and keep going. Don't overshoot your mark with impossible goals—be realistic each step upward. Never doubt or do anything that denies you from getting what you want. Know that everything is working for your own good, regardless of what transpires in your life. You will demonstrate in the direction your thoughts run. Believe that you will be, and are, successful. Accept it as if it were true. Thank

God in advance for bringing you the things you want. Be positive at all times. Take action. Be persistent; it is the number one key to success. J. Paul Getty, Sr., was one of the world's richest men—a billionaire! He patiently waited out for twenty years to buy out all of the stockholders so he would be in complete control. His persistence paid off. Try to remember, in your pursuit of riches, that "Rome wasn't built in a day."

You may start small, i.e., own a hot dog stand. Then you may take the money earned and invest in a small shop and eventually own a chain of stores. When you expand you are confident that you are doing well and know that you are going to do better. Thoughts of expansion attract wealth. Ari Onassis started out by selling cigars in the streets, and he gradually invested in bigger things, i.e., a fleet of ships and an airline, etc., he was always demonstrating(thinking in a visual manner) for more. He was never satisfied with what he had. Dolly Parton in an interview for *TV GUIDE* magazine (October 17, 1987 issue) said about her success, "It all came from wanting more. I'll always be too much for some people, but I'll never be enough for me." In the same interview she remarked, "I like to take my negatives and turn them into positives." She has a relentless-positive-thinking and faith-in-herself attitude. She's a Capricorn who knows how to be a super rich and famous star!

Often it's difficult to be a positive thinker. It may take working at. Your mind gets set in a groove and then it's a struggle to break a habit; however, it's not impossible. When you try to change habits, do it **one step at a time**. If you try to rush with too many changes, confusion results and then you may be right back at the place you started from.

The thoughts you send out constitute the process known as "demonstrating"—which means thinking your thoughts into existence. This holds true when you hide (plant) *seed money* or write the *Law of Abundance check*, and so forth. Like attracts like; you attract what is in your mind. Start off by saying, "I love myself." When you love yourself it is easier to attract the things you want. If you have a strong drive for power, success and wealth, it's the love of yourself that spurns you on. Often, a loved one may inspire you to make your fortune. It's vital that you have faith in yourself and in your own judgment. Be ready to take a stand—firm but not abrasive—if you believe in your ideas and plans. Learn to be your own supportive coach; however be tough on yourself when necessary. Don't brood over failures or setbacks; know that to err is human.

Try to think that you *are* as good as the top person in your field; that you can win in every test. Tell yourself, "I can conquer anything." Do your best and don't worry about the consequences. Know that you tried. If you don't take chances, you'll always wonder what might have been. Know that you can go to the heights because **you have the power within you** to do so. Because you **know** success exists, it **does** exist. Be determined. Don't let anything interfere with your efforts to succeed. Do not allow anyone to sway you from your goals. If necessary make personal sacrifices (most of the time you have to when you want to win the brass ring). Don't be afraid to set your foot on the highest hill to get to the top. Believe within that there's nothing you can't do to become rich and successful.

Do not say, "I am poor," or you'll be poor. Instead say, "I am rich and getting richer. I am successful and getting more successful. I am lucky and getting luckier." Make a list of your past successes and update it. Review, from time to time, what you have accomplished. When you do tune in to your past successes, it reinforces your courage and gives you the incentive to top yourself. Also, your self-esteem is raised. Sometimes, you may forget about all of your wonderful accomplishments and get into a negative rut that pulls you downward. Thus when you refer to your "Success List," it keeps you positive. If you have failed at one or more projects, consider yourself as having a few setbacks that were temporary situations. One failure doesn't make you a failure. The majority of the rich and famous have all had one or more failures in their lifetime but they didn't get discouraged; instead, they kept trying until they were again in the winner's circle. So, why can't you do the same?

Are you aware that your mind cannot think two thoughts simultaneously? Therefore, use control and dwell on the positive. Thus you eliminate the negative. Try to think about a single harmonious thought as long as you can, such as, "I AM successful." This puts your thinking in the affirmative and present tense, thereby making your desire a reality that much quicker. Look for the good in situations and people. Don't limit yourself. Avoid small and petty thoughts. Think big and you'll be big. "What you think is what you attract," is an adage that the ancients recognized as truth.

Eliminate the words, "I can't" and "I won't" from your vocabulary. Don't even think these thoughts. If you say, "I won't get that raise, promotion, money desired, etc., — you won't because you've put out the thought that you won't. But be patient, you may not get what you want overnight.

If you find that your mind is in a negative rut, try to develop positive thoughts. Use my *Mirror* "magical device" and give yourself a "pep-talk" in front of the mirror. Tell yourself, "You are talented and are going to get the job you want. You are successful. You are a great actor. You are magnetic. You are gutsy. You are happy, confident and intelligent." Always say **you** when you talk to yourself in front of a mirror.

What type of person do you want to be? Create an image and always keep that image in mind. Act and believe as if you **are** that person. Dare to be original. Don't hold back on ideas. Let people know about them, especially the boss. Others may oppose some of your views but be persistent, logical and practical in your presentation. If one set of people say that you are too ahead of the times, don't be afraid to take your projects elsewhere. Never give up. Believe in yourself and others will believe in you. Seek new opportunities. Solve your problems, that of the boss or community. If you discover a procedure that improves your job, speak out and offer to install or supervise the new program or system.

Do not be afraid of success—afraid that you'll have to sacrifice fun, family, love, friends and other things to achieve it. However, don't get the idea that sacrifice isn't involved, because it is. How much you deny yourself depends upon how high your aims are—the higher the goals, the bigger the sacrifices are to reach them. Perhaps, you will have to forego wasting valuable time and stop watching television, or goofing off with your pals. Partying may come to a standstill unless it's for business purposes. Your exercise program and sports activities may have to be cut down and more time spent on work-related projects. Overwork. Do more than you have to. Go that extra mile. Take on more than you can handle. Be so busy that you don't have time to think about anything negative.

Take on many responsibilities. Keep busy. If others want to idle, let them—but don't copy your friends if they are lackadaisical. Don't give up in despair. Practice self-denial when necessary to achieve a goal. Don't feel sorry for yourself in the process. Be industrious, and have singleness of purpose. Formulate a plan and don't stop until you've accomplished it. Keep your ideas to yourself, if you are the boss, you don't want them stolen. Don't gripe, complain, worry, or be suspicious. Discipline your subconscious mind to follow a positive road. Prepare for success and you'll achieve it. Don't criticize or you'll be criticized. Feed your ego with a winning attitude. Be grateful for your abilities and put them to use in every way you possible can. Program your mind so that only good will happen. Don't kill your dreams and opportunities by belittling others and their ideas. Be open-minded. Realize that you are the most important person in your life. When you love yourself, you feel good and in return others will love you too.

Do not make up excuses in the form of alibis by saying, "I can't do—" or "I am misunder-stood," or "No one understands me," "If only I had the time to pursue my ideas," or "She had connections and I didn't," or "I'd be happy if I had married—," or "Society is to blame for—," or "I can't get hired because the economy is bad," or"I wouldn't be so lonely if others were more friendly." By expressing this type of negative energy, you could be holding yourself back from the life you've always yearned for. Make it a practice to eliminate all negative words from your vocabulary when talking to yourself or others.

If you are married and working long hours and sacrificing personal pleasures, encourage your mate to keep busy. Try to get your wife involved in charity work, fund raising, a regular job or other activities that interest her. Then she won't complain about your never being home much and your marriage will have a better chance of lasting. If you are married and working overtime, try to push your husband to do the same. Otherwise if he tries to hold you back from attaining your goals, you could be headed for the divorce courts. Or if you decide to save your marriage and give up your career-dreams, you may regret it to such a point that you develop health problems....and you wallow in self-pity over your miserable life. Years later, you may give up your partner and enter the career work field—hopefully, it won't be too late. If you are both workaholic's your marriage has a good chance of surviving. If both of your work hours coincide, you'll be making more money and the sacrifices will be by both parties. This action helps keep the marriage together even though you may be apart in the process. If your husband *is not* an overachiever, and you are, then try to encourage him in active and competitive sports or a hobby that will keep him occupied while you are working overtime.

Plan, prepare and work hard—these are the three requisites for getting to the top, although talent is necessary too. It takes effort, not just wishful thinking. Daydreaming expends energy so put action behind those dreams. Make them be a reality. Be confident that you'll get the success you want. Confidence and enthusiasm go hand-in-hand to attract wealth, and the other things you want, i.e., love, marriage, children. A high-level of enthusiasm is always infectious and can help create a positive home and work environment. The winners, who gamble or are involved in athletics, are confident and enthusiastic. They know that Lady Luck is smiling at them or a Gold medal is going to hang around their neck.

Have you ever been on a shopping spree and kept spending money like water was going through your hands? Do you recall the enthusiasm you felt? Didn't you feel as if you were on a roll? You might have said, "I'm not going to worry about money. I feel rich today. There will be more where this is coming from. I know that I will always have it. So why not spend it?" It is this confident and enthusiastic attitude that keeps the money rolling in your direction. The moment you stop and penny pinch the flow stops. Therefore the next time you go shopping, regardless of how much or little you spend, tell yourself, "I am going to get more money and more money, so it's okay to spend now. I am rich and getting richer. There's money out there in the world and it is waiting for me. There's no reason in the world why I can't get it." Be sure and put **strong** and **emotional feelings**, with **intense enthusiasm**, into your thoughts. This is important to do every time you demonstrate for a particular thing.

After money is received say, "Thank you for giving me this money. You can also say (*before money is received*), "Thank you in advance for giving me this money." You may ask, "Who am I thanking?" Perhaps, it is God, the Creator, a Supreme Being, Supreme Power or Your Inner Self. It is an inner feeling that lets you know that you have Divine Protection and are being provided for. Hasn't the Creator provided you with a home, food or job? So why should the Creator stop? It's your negative thoughts that make things come to a temporary standstill. By the way, when you ask for money, do not state an amount because you could receive more than anticipated. Never limit yourself to stated sums.

It is very spiritual to love money as long as you keep it in circulation. You are keeping the grocer, tailor, shop owner, theatre, restaurant, etc. in business. If you are an employer, you are helping your employees earn money so they can feed and shelter their families. If you are a miser, you are only helping yourself—and that is selfish.

Never be envious of the riches or good luck that another person has. If someone you know gets a lot of money, regardless of where it comes from—inheritance, raise, lottery, law suit—say, and mean it, "That's wonderful. He/she deserves it. I wish for him/her to get even more." When you send out this type of thought, it bounces back at you. If you say the reverse, that also will bounce back at you. So be happy for another's good fortune.

You cannot praise people, or yourself, too much or too often. Let people know you appreciate their efforts and in return they will appreciate yours. It is very important that you praise yourself. Say, "I praise myself for being confident, outgoing, cheerful, enthusiastic, and positive." Or, "I praise myself for accomplishing my goals." Start telling yourself good things about yourself. Send impersonal love thoughts to others. Buy *love* postage stamps and mail your letters, bills, with that *love* stamp. Send out love to the world. When you put the stamp on the envelope, and in the mail box, say, "I bless you and send impersonal love, prosperity and happiness to you."

Keep mentally and physically active. Ask for bigger and better things. Don't be afraid to request the biggest and finest of everything. And why not? Be good to yourself. See things grander and larger than they really are. Look at life through rose-colored glasses. Feel and know that there's always **more** for you. Never let go of the mental image you have. **State** what you want, **believe** you have it and **know** that it is yours. Think only about what you want, not lack. If you want a radio, picture it in your home. See your refrigerators and cupboards filled with groceries. Visualize yourself living the lifestyles of the rich and famous. If you watch the television show of the same name, say, "That's me there at the beach, hotel, restaurant and fur or jewelry store." *Imagine at that moment* that you are really there and traveling all over the world. Write the tourist bureaus to send you free travel folders. Study them when they arrive. Make believe you are going to those exotic places. Pretend you have expensive luggage, clothes, jewels, furs, cars or a mansion.

Know that what you want is coming to you as fast as you can receive it. Realize that love, money and possessions are there waiting for you. Do **not** set a time limit or amount on anything. Hold the mental picture of what you want in your thoughts with the fixed purpose to get what you want, and the unwavering faith that you will have it. Close your mind against all that may tend to shake your purpose, dim your vision, or quench your belief.

Perhaps, you may want to do like Frank Sinatra did when he was young and just getting started. He purchased expensive clothes to make a good impression so people would think he's rich. This is **Demonstration** at its best. He was confident that he would be rich someday. Frank told it to others. Perhaps, you also will want to gradually buy expensive clothes, accessories or home furnishings and replace the inexpensive apparel ,or objects, with luxurious ones. Get excited with each new purchase. It is this feeling of wealth that attracts riches. Pretend the desired possession is already yours. Don't say you are going to buy it with your next paycheck because that's limiting where the actual cash is coming from. What if you won a Bingo or lottery contest? — the money could be coming from there. Say, "I don't know how, or where, the money is coming from, but I KNOW that I am going to have it to buy —."

Be happy, cheerful, friendly and have a smile for everyone. If you don't feel very gleeful, buy a joke book and read a joke, or more, a day. Pretend you are an actor and this is a part that you are going to play—the happy-go-lucky role. Laughter is contagious; people want to be in your company and it helps attract money. There are two delicatessen's in New York City on the same block. One owner is outgoing, the other an introvert. The busiest deli is the one with the shop owner who always has a smile on his face, and it is more expensive than the other deli. It just goes to show you that some people will pay a higher price just to have some good cheer spread their way. There are others who patronize the cheaper place, and the customers there are serious like the owner; they prefer his cheap prices. However, I heard that he may be going out of business soon because his income has decreased substantially.

Think big but do be a little realistic. See what *you want to see*. Refuse to think of anything negative. Often you have to lie to yourself to make it a reality and then, later, the unreal becomes real. If something appears to be bad, don't give it additional energy by thinking about it. Instead say, "I am lucky and getting luckier. My good is everywhere. I move to my greater good." This type of affirmation keeps the mind positive. Every desire (thought) regardless of how small is energy that can be used toward accomplishment or destruction. When creative imagination is used, various mental images are brought into combination. Ideas and plans are thus formulated and they are built in the mind. Once physical action is taken, you set them into motion.

Your way of doing things is the result of the manner you think about things. Form what you want in thought and impress your thought upon formless substance, thus causing the things you think about to be created. You may want to meditate or go into a trance. However, if you spend too much time in meditation, there won't be much time to accomplish things. If you daydream too much, you also dissipate energy for accomplishment. It's good to have dreams but you must put your dreams into action. Because without action, there's no movement; you are holding on to the energy instead of letting it out.

Be gutsy, pushy, enterprising and go after the things you want. Be persistent. Don't allow anyone to interfere with your plans or schedule. Say "no" to people that want you to goof off partying. Tend to business. Don't let any problem stop you from going after your goals.

Say, "I am going to get this." Do not give up. Know that it is yours. To attract wealth tell yourself, "I've got to hurry. I have so many projects to attend to. Everything great is happening to me so fast that I've got to keep up with it all." Constructive action can produce affirmative results. Put your whole mind into your present operations. Don't wait for things to happen. Act now!

There are two types of people in the following example: one tends to be a winner, the other a loser. Bill is aggressive, talkative, always in a hurry and moves fast. His business is booming. Bill's office is like Grand Central Station. He is talking on two phones, has a client seated at his desk and is smiling in spite of all the chaos. Joe is calm, cool, collected, quiet, nonaggressive and moves slow. His business is almost at a standstill. Joe's office is neat, tidy and noiseless. A client comes in the room and Joe takes forever to discuss projects. What is wrong? Bill's mind is fast, thus business is prospering. Joe's mind is slow, thus business is barely crawling. It is the go-go-go type like Bill who is successful, because he rushes hurriedly about and has his fingers in so many projects that he has to move fast to accomplish his tasks. Joe doesn't have hardly any deals; therefore, he can take his time and go at a snail's pace. Joe needs to get his mind busier, and do some exercises to be more agile, and be gutsy and take action by going into new lines of endeavor because he is stagnating. If

Bill continues at his fast rate, he'll be rich quickly. If Joe continues at his slow rate, he may be out of business sooner than he'd like.

Customers go where there is action. In New York City, Bloomingdale's department store does a very good business. It is a lively place with plenty of hustle, bustle; there are television sets on different floors showing a designers latest fashion, etc. The store is elegant, noisy and crowded; and people are there spending money. The public doesn't tend to go to quiet places; they go where there's movement—action. In such an environment they move slowly out of the store because of the interesting activity going on from floor to floor. However in a place that is half empty, a customer may be in and out of the store in a jiffy. Thus he/she may pass the merchandise quickly and not be tempted to buy anything. In a crowded store a person has time to see everything because people don't move very fast. The empty place is devoid of noise and customers; therefore, it is not making money like the store swarming with people. **The public goes where the action is**; therefore, if you own a business—move the merchandise around, put some music in, or television shows depicting the products, or hire live demonstrators who cook, do make up etc., to sell the merchandise.

To be rich: find a need and fulfill it. Look around you and see what type of business is lacking in your area. Perhaps it is a service, a manufactured item, a product that is new, doesn't exist (something you may invent) or that is a short cut and time saver for the user. There is money out there to be made. You've got to think of the need. Could you sew, bake or cook something that is unique? Start it, make it a winner and then franchise it with your logo. Visit New York City and walk the streets; perhaps there is something in New York that you could make a fortune with in your home town.

Once your venture starts booming, put your earnings back into the business. Do not spend it on yourself or on vacations, furs, jewelry, a new wardrobe, wining and dining in expensive restaurants—that's eating up your capital and profits. A sign for success is taking that money and reinvesting it in new equipment, machines, computers, merchandise, advertising, etc., that will speed up—and improve—production. Also your corporation should invest in real estate, eventually own apartment buildings, and be a landlord. Invest in something like money-market funds; the interest received from them could go into property or some foolish spending.

Pay yourself the lowest salary you can afford to live on, at least for the first year or two of your business. Let your corporation pay your rent, buy a car in the company's name--not yours. Don't expand too fast. Just because you are doing great, don't start moving to larger quarters. Reap the profits and expand gradually.

Ask an accountant or financial adviser before you make any big moves.

Continually keep your mind OPEN to new avenues of making money, to a better job, expansion, or going up the ladder to the top. Say, "I am brilliant and doing a great job"—you'll see the results. Whenever you praise yourself for being a particular way, you'll become that person. Think about what you want on a daily basis; also, WANT what you think. That's just what you'll get—no more, no less.

Money is an essential sign for success. Those entrepreneur's who are into big money tend to have it pouring in from many different avenues. A smart business man/woman never puts all of his/ her eggs into one basket. He/she branches out into various enterprises. It is good to diversify. For instance, perhaps you are a teacher—you might get involved in writing, publishing your own pamphlets, start up a radio show about the subject you teach, sell items that you manufacture in connection with what you are doing—the possibilities are endless.

Plot, plan and think, "How else can I get money?" Be ambitious. Think, "I am not doing enough." Always strive for more. Don't hurt others in the process of going after wealth. Remember, whatever you do, it will bounce back to you. Instead of mentally or physically spending money, put it into the bank and let it accumulate. Then spend on the necessities; however, you've got to have some fun and be good to yourself so buy yourself something you really want. Or go on a short vacation. Many overachievers feel that making money is their pleasure and they dislike taking time away from the business. Once you are relaxing on a trip, it is difficult to get back in the "money groove" again because you may still be in the "fun groove.

Don't say you are saving money for a rainy day. Instead say, "I am saving money for future investments and a good time." Help others in distress. Donate money to good causes. Keep in mind that when you do, it will bounce back to you. Share the wealth and watch your money increase in unlimited and staggering sums. Feel that you are rich and that you are making others wealthy and conferring benefits to all. Don't talk about past financial or love problems. Avoid thoughts of poverty. Only think of wealth, love, marriage, happiness and success. Whenever you think, or speak, of those who are poor—think of them as rich or becoming wealthy; this includes the entire world. Anytime you can help motivate another through encouragement, do so. Spread money around. Trust others and delegate jobs; this aids in motivating them, which can be a valuable resource saving you time and money. Delegating things allows you the freedom to do bigger and better projects. There is room for everyone to make a buck. Not one individual or company could handle all of the business.

Often a person will say, "I am too old to do anything new or to start a business." However, age didn't stop Grandma Moses from painting and it hasn't stopped Barbara Cartland from writing romance novels, designing, traveling and promoting. When you are busy, you don't have time to complain, feel sorry for yourself, get lonely or depressed. The idea is to keep so busy that you don't have time to get into this rut of negativity. Smile, cheer people up, donate time to church bazaars, or be active with the senior citizens or serve meals to the needy. Help others like Mother Theresa. Don't sit around the house wasting valuable time watching television. Be active. Avoid selfishness. Watch your money increase.

Work at a part time job. Have several jobs. If your attention is occupied constructively on being active in various projects, you won't be getting an audience of people listening to you whine and whimper. Instead, you'll get people around you who will compliment you for your wonderful attributes. And just think about how great those praises will make you feel!

Don't allow your emotions to run away with you. Chase the blues away by being active, or watch happy shows on television, at the theatre or in a movie house. Avoid tear-jerker plots. Watch shows that make you laugh or think. Play games. Be carefree. Put emotional joy into your life. Take up a hobby. Go to lectures or sporting events. Go to school. I have a client who has been going to college since he was eighty-five years old; he's now ninety three years old. During his working years, he was too busy to study the subjects which interested him. Therefore, he's now taking a history course which, when finished, will be followed by a language course!

Avoid thoughts of failure. Instead compensate the feeling of inadequacy by appearing confident. Shine and show off so others will not know that inside you are insecure. The majority of successful people from every line of endeavor have, at one time, expressed an inferiority complex. However, their egos were so strong that they compensated by showing a superiority complex. So, if you fall into this category, just think—you are in good company with top celebrities, politicians, industrialists and world leaders. Don't brag or boast about your success because this action makes others resent you and, thus, send you negative vibrations.

Don't devote all of your time with one project or client. Diversify by having many ventures and, thus, increase your clientele. Thus you release the energy so money will come to you from various enterprises. Then if something falls through, you won't be too upset because you've still got many irons in the fire. If you get into a situation where you are extremely disturbed, say, "I am forever undisturbed. I have divine protection. The creator will provide a solution to my problem."

What do you do about the shocks that occur through other people? What should you do when you get fired or laid off of a job? Often you may get shook up by a change, and are thrown for a loop in the process. Regardless of the situation, tell yourself, "Everything happens for the best. It happened because it was meant to be. There is something better coming my way." Look for a new job in another field. It's time for a change. Work a part time job in the interim. Start your own business. Perhaps, independence is desired. Usually ten years later, a person will say, "I am sure glad I got fired when I did. If it had not happened, I wouldn't be here making all of this money." Often, a change is to get you out of a rut. It wakes you up! Have faith, expect that good will come, pray and ask help from God.

Try to adjust to outer changes but keep cool within. Don't allow conditions, situations or people to affect you. If you permit it, usually problems are attracted. Realize that all experience, good or bad, has a lesson to be learned and is thus valuable if you look at it that way. Try to rearrange your thoughts, feelings and actions. Thus you'll be better equipped to handle yourself and those with whom you come into contact. Often you may think it is easier to blame outside conditions for your difficulties than it is to blame yourself. However if you realize that it is YOU who is attracting the condition, this will be half the battle and may help end the thought that you are subject to whatever occurs. Never allow yourself to feel disappointed. You may expect to have a certain thing at a specific time; hold to your faith you will receive it, or something better. Always speak in terms of advancement. Create what you want and you are above fear.

Have you ever gone on a job interview and been rejected? If so, did you come home and cry and, practically, give up for the moment? Or did you take a positive approach? If you are turned down for a job, it is in your best interest to mentally say, "Thank you. You did me a favor. There will be a better job offered with more money, prestige or recognition. " Thus, armed with **this** attitude, you have a better chance of attracting a fabulous job--one that could, possibly, take you all the way to the top! Don't sit at home waiting for a job interview. Take action and see about many occupations. If you aren't out there, how will a potential employer know you exist? Do not concern yourself with questions to how you shall surmount obstacles which may come. **Pretend** there are NO obstacles. Never admit to the possibility of failure or speak in a way that infers failure as a possibility.

If people start in with "The times are bad," answer with, "I really don't want to discuss it. Never speak of business conditions as being doubtful. People made fortunes during the depression. There's money out there to make, even in a recession." The people who did get rich during the depression were positive thinkers. They took advantage of the opportunities. It is not good for you to listen to complaints about"the hard times," because then you will tend to dwell on it and the next thing you may wonder is, "Why am I having money problems?"

Avoid calling friends, loved ones or relatives with an emotional, "I don't know how I will survive." "My business is terrible." "The telephone doesn't ring." "I have only a few customers." "I'm not making any money." "I lost my job." Actually you want someone's sympathy when you make this type of phone call. If you put out the thought that you are NOT doing well, the other individual is going to give you a bad mental treatment without realizing it. Because that person is going to think about your lack of funds, that mental treatment is going to make things even tighter for you(thoughts produce things). If people ask you, "How is business?" Answer with, "I'm busy. Everything is fine." Then, you'll be sent a positive mental treatment and soon it will come true. Avoid saturating others with your negative and frustrated emotions. If you do need advice then state your problem in a calm, cool and collected manner.

If you are going out on an interview, it's best to keep it to yourself. You don't want anyone to send you negative thoughts relative to that interview. If you are an actor or actress and are going out on audition calls, don't tell anyone about it until you've signed a contract for the part. If anyone asks you if you are working or going on auditions, answer with, "I'm so busy I don't have time to talk about it."

I do not allow anyone to put negative vibrations into my walls. Therefore, I will not allow people to be depressed in my presence. There are ways to cheer people up. Be funny with a story. Keep their minds detracted from themselves and on something entirely different. When they do manage to speak negatively, I try to find something pleasing about them and cheer them up with a compliment. I let them know that things are never as bad as they appear, They have the power within them to change, or channel, their negative thoughts into constructive ones.

If you move to a new place, or no longer are living with someone who was negative—perhaps, you will want to cleanse the walls of negative energy. Burn sandalwood incense and simultaneously carry it around so the walls will be saturated with the smoke and while so doing, recite THE LORD'S PRAYER. Keep light colors—pale rose or yellow—on the walls or in your decor. The more sunny and light your rooms are, the more sunny and light you'll be.

Now that you've made it to the top, perhaps you are thinking, "I should retire." Or if you're an actor you may say, "I've been working so hard that I think I'll take a year off." If you take time off, you'll wonder why your telephone isn't ringing for work. If you retire, you may wonder why your money is suddenly dwindling down. Or if you say, "When I win the lottery, I'll quit my job." Quitting and retiring is not in your best interest unless you have plenty of money invested and working for you. Otherwise, if you live off of your savings, you'll really get depressed when the money gradually disappears.

When your mind stops growing for money, your money also stops growing. In the beginning when you started your climb to the top of the ladder of success, you were obsessed to make money and be in a high position. Your persistence and talent took you up to a certain plateau. However, it seemed like you couldn't get beyond this level. Why? You know that all of that wealth is so near but it seems to elude you. Why? It is all very simple. You became comfortable with the bigger money but in your contentment you were no longer compelled to work overtime or to go out of your way to get richer. Once you became satisfied, you didn't strive anymore. If you want to be super rich, you can't be content with what you've got. You must WANT MORE like Dolly Parton and all of the wealthy entrepreneurs. You must continue, **at every moment,** to build an empire. Don't let your mind stop growing or your money will stop growing. It is that simple.

The level of accomplishment that you want to attain has to be decided upon by you, and you alone. It is what makes YOU happy—these are all signs for success. Think of yourself as building a house—a money house—and each